The Mormon Graphic Image

I met a man named Jonas Ives,
Who loved & cherished 7 wives,
Every wife had 7 sons,
Every son had 7 wives.
Wives, sons, sons & wives:
     Think of the troubles of Jonas Ives!

The Mormon Graphic Image, 1834–1914

CARTOONS, CARICATURES, and ILLUSTRATIONS

Gary L. Bunker and Davis Bitton

University of Utah Press

Salt Lake City   1983

Volume Sixteen of the University of Utah Publications
in the American West under the editorial direction of
the American West Center.
S. Lyman Tyler, Director
Brigham D. Madsen, General Editor

© 1983 University of Utah Press, Salt Lake City 84112
Printed in the United States of America

Library of Congress Cataloging in Publication Data

Bunker, Gary L., 1934–
    The Mormon graphic image, 1834–1914.

    (University of Utah publications in the American
West; v. 16)
    Bibliography: p.
    Includes index.
    1. Mormons—Caricatures and cartoons.   2. Mormons—
Controversial literature.   I. Bitton, Davis, 1930–
II. Title.   III. Series.
    BX8638.B86   1983   289.3′022′2   83–1305
    ISBN 0-87480-218-0

Frontispiece. Jonas Ives. *Life*, 22 November 1906.

Contents

Illustrations

Preface

Two nineteenth-century cartoons on the Mormons in John and Selma Appel's *The Distorted Image*, a publication of the Anti-Defamation League of B'nai Brith, triggered this study of the popular graphic image of Mormonism. Similar studies on the images of blacks, native Americans, Catholics, and Jews have highlighted the visual stereotypes that shaped and reflected public opinion toward these groups. Since this area of historical research on Mormonism has been virtually ignored, a parallel scholarly analysis seemed long overdue. Just as the scholarly publications on the images of other religious and ethnic minorities examined prejudicial propaganda, so is this work intended to illuminate the roots of misunderstanding and misrepresentation.

In 1974 our search through almanacs, illustrated books, illustrated periodicals, newspapers, separately published prints, song sheet covers, broadsides, and other sources began. The collection phase started, naturally enough, with the materials housed in the fine repositories of the State of Utah. One year later the quest expanded to the Library of Congress, the New York Public Library, The New-York Historical Society, Princeton, Yale, Harvard, the Boston Public Library, the Boston Museum of Fine Arts, the American Antiquarian Society, and the California State Public Library at Sacramento.

Since the initial investigative thrust, several other sources have been searched. A trip to the University of Texas at Austin introduced us to *Texas Siftings*. The Charles Redd Fellowship for Western History financed another few weeks on the East Coast. *American Punch, Frank Leslie's Budget of Fun, New York Picayune, New Varieties, Nick Nax, Sam the Scaramouch, Thistleton's Jolly Giant, Wild Oats,* and other obscure sources augmented our collection of visual artifacts. During the summer of 1979 the Western Reserve Historical Society in Cleveland yielded new finds. When we could not thumb through the primary resources ourselves we were obligated to resort to other methods. A librarian at the University of Illinois at Urbana–Champaign, Doria M. Beachell, searched the files of *Phunny Phellow* and the *Arkansaw Traveler*. Correspondence with specialists in related fields also uncovered rich material. Finally, the convenience of the interlibrary loans of microfilm revealed the mood of Mormon cartoons from the pages of newspapers in the 1890s and 1900s.

Such extensive research would not have been possible without generous financial support. Our major benefactor was Brigham Young University. These funds were allocated and administered by the College of Family, Home, and Social Sciences, The Charles Redd Center for Western History, and the Harold B. Lee Library (which becomes the repository of our collection). We are also grateful to the Mormon History Fund.

Numerous individuals have helped us along the way. John and Selma Appel gave us the inspiration for the research and then offered helpful suggestions and encouragement. Chad Flake pointed the way to the extensive Mormon book and periodical literature. Leonard Arrington read the final manuscript. Martin Hickman, Dean of the College of Family, Home, and Social Sciences at Brigham Young University, managed to find funding for travel when the standard sources had been exhausted. Carol B. Bunker gave special encouragement. Many others including devoted research assistants, secretaries, and numerous library specialists across the country made their mark on the project. To these we express appreciation while absolving them from any defects in the final product, for which we assume full responsibility.

In a large project of this kind, in addition to amassing the visual and textual exidence, we have found it advantageous to present specific portions in the classroom, in public lectures, and in a few instances in published articles. We are grateful to the following for allowing us to repeat in this book all or parts of articles previously published or in press: *Prints of the American West; Brigham Young University Studies; Dialogue: A Journal of Mormon Thought; Utah Historical Quarterly;* and *Sunstone.*

And of course we are grateful to the University of Utah Press for recognizing the signficance of the project, for sharing our vision of a quality publication, and for excellent editorial and design assistance.

The Mormon Graphic Image

Introduction

This study of the Mormon image, as it was presented in illustrations between 1834 and 1914, can best be understood within the context of Mormon history.[1] As an organized movement, the Church of Jesus Christ of Latter-day Saints (to use the name it soon acquired and carries to the present) came into existence in upstate New York in 1830. Its founder was Joseph Smith, a young man of twenty-five years. The Mormons saw their church as quintessentially Christian; after a millennium and a half of apostasy—a distortion and corruption of the doctrinal truths of Christianity and, even more fatal, the consequent loss of sacerdotal authority—the true and living church of Christ had been restored to earth by divine intervention. New scriptures and modern revelations combined with the Bible to guide the Latter-day Saints, and these gave answers to questions about heaven and earth, about cosmic meaning and present obligations, about the past and future, and about political and economic issues.

This general restorationist stance put the Mormons outside of the denominational consensus, and such views made them objects of scorn and derision. Multiple factors, including prejudice from elements of the local populace and lack of wisdom on the part of some of the Latter-day Saints, intensified the persecution. So it was that they moved from place to place seeking a refuge. Upstate New York, central Ohio, western Missouri, western Illinois—these were the successive centers of the Mormon "gathering." In each place there was opposition, which culminated in the martyrdom of Joseph and Hyrum Smith and the flight of the outcasts from the state of Illinois. After an epic migration across the plains of Iowa and Nebraska and a wintering near present-day Omaha, the Saints pushed on to the Great Basin and there, in the Salt Lake Valley, established a refuge.

By 1850 the Mormon image was generally unfavorable. Members had a reputation for being lower-class, superstitious dupes. Their leaders were seen as frauds and connivers. The religion was ridiculed.[2] At times, however, they did evoke some sympathy and benefited from benevolent friends. The persecu-

---

1. A good one-volume survey is James B. Allen and Glen M. Leonard, *The Story of the Latter-day Saints* (Salt Lake City: Deseret Book Co., 1976).

2. See chapter on "Early Persecutions," in Leonard J. Arrington and Davis Bitton, *The Mormon Experience: A History of the Latter-day Saints* (New York: Knopf, 1979).

tion represented one side of the popular reaction, while expressions of concern and charitable aid represented the other side.[3]

In a new location, recognized as a territory, the Latter-day Saints hoped to be left peaceably to follow their own ways. But when the practice of polygamy was publicly acknowledged in 1852, the popular view rapidly wound itself around the negative pole. For the next forty years, with an ebb and flow of intensity, the Mormons were the object of a campaign seeking to force an end to their system of plural marriage. Their political and economic practices—bloc voting and different kinds of communitarianism—also aroused opposition. The campaign against Mormonism proceeded on different levels. The clergy and other spokespersons led reform campaigns. There were legislative enactments and judicial decisions. Hence, Mormon Utah was a favorite subject of comment in newspapers and magazines. Their leader Brigham Young (and his successors), their polygamy, their economic programs, their system of gathering new converts —all these were pilloried.

The year 1890 has traditionally been seen as a major demarcation in Mormon history, for it was then that polygamy was officially discontinued. In actuality the change of fortune did not happen all at once. Opposition was weakened by the issuance of a manifesto by church President Wilford Woodruff announcing that plural marriages were no longer being performed. In 1896 Utah entered the Union as a state. Some of the old questions and lingering suspicions continued on, however, especially during the years 1898–1900 (when Mormon leader B. H. Roberts was elected to the national Congress and, after a committee investigation, denied his seat because he was a polygamist), 1903–7 (when Apostle Reed Smoot was elected to the U.S. Senate and, after another investigation, allowed to take his seat), and 1908–10 (when the anti-Mormon American Party won local elections in Utah and stimulated journalistic muckraking charges against the church). But by and large the Latter-day Saints were slowly moving into a position of general respectability.

These broad outlines remind us that from the beginning Mormonism was an unpopular minority. In the interplay between Mormons and the larger society consideration must be given both to what the Mormons were doing and to the impression they created in the minds of others. Their image, to use today's fashionable word, was itself part of the drama. To study that image—the way in which Mormons were perceived by others—can be done on different levels and by means of different kinds of evidence, such as novels, periodicals, or travel litera-

3. See, for example, Davis Bitton, "American Philanthropy and Mormon Refugees, 1846–1849," *Journal of Mormon History* 7 (1980):63–81.

ture. Some of the scholarship that considers such things has already accumulated.[4]

What has not yet been studied with any thoroughness are the popular graphic images. Occasionally samples of cartoons based on Mormonism have appeared in books or articles, but there has been no systematic examination of the entire corpus of visual representations. Assuming that pictures were themselves a major source of the popular image people had of the Mormons, we have thought it worth our while to collect them, analyze them, and write the present work in an attempt to understand them. So setting out the chronological boundaries of 1834, when the first print about Mormons was published, and 1914, when World War I ushered in a new phase, we have accumulated all pictures we could find with Mormons as their subject. We have excluded photographs, paintings, simple portraits, and pictures of landscapes or buildings. Even after the delimitation there remain several hundred published pictures—line drawings of different kinds reproduced by various forms of print technology —that did much, we believe, to establish the images most people had in their heads when thinking about Mormons. We have structured our text so that the initial chapters deal with the chronological development of the Mormon image in the media from 1834 to 1914. In Part II we examine in detail particular aspects of the Mormon image in relation to individual topics.

Some may question the value of recovering these pictorial artifacts from the dusty pages of history. We are aware of the argument "that it [is] best to disregard . . . attacks in picture and print so as not to give wider publicity to verbal and iconographic calumnies."[5] Yet, we are persuaded by recent image histories of blacks, native Americans, Jews, Catholics, and others that these works have exposed, not strengthened, the prejudices of the past.[6] In so doing they enrich the appreciation of the victimized as they strip away the layers of stereotype.

It is through a careful examination of primary materials like these pictures that we begin to understand why it was that the Mormons of the past century felt themselves so beleaguered and

---

4. Allen and Leonard, *The Story of the Latter-day Saints*, p. 648.

5. John J. Appel, "Popular Graphics as Documents for Teaching and Studying Jewish History," in *A Bicentennial Festschrift for Jacob Rader Marius*, Bertram Wallace Korn, ed. (New York: KTAV Publishing House, Inc., 1976).

6. See Winthrop D. Jordan, *The White Man's Burden* (New York: Oxford University Press, 1974); Robert F. Berkhofer, *The White Man's Indian* (New York: Alfred A. Knopf, 1978); George M. Fredrickson, *The Black Image in the White Mind* (New York: Harper and Row, 1971); Rudolph Glanz, *The Jew in Early American Wit and Graphic Humor* (New York: KTAV Publishing House, Inc., 1973); and John and Selma Appel, "The Grand Old Sport of Hating Catholics," *The Critic* (November–December 1971):50–58.

why it was that many people with little or no direct contact with Mormons could be so unfriendly. "What fools these mortals be!" Erasmus of Rotterdam's quip suggests a way of approaching the material—as a case study of human groups in interaction. Going through these many illustrations gives one an education in the nature of stereotyping, something not easily obtained by a verbal definition. One discovers how to be aware of the process—and why we should beware of it.

We know that many other groups suffered from similar image problems. Blacks, native Americans, immigrants of different nationalities, other religious groups, even such a large "minority" as women, all suffered from the dual process of stereotyping followed by unfair, cruel treatment. The Mormons were not the only victims, but their experience is the subject of the present book. From it perhaps principles with broad application can be learned.

PART I

The Development of the Visual Image

I. Shaping the Visual Image, 1830–1869

"Many false reports, lies and foolish stories were published in the newspapers,"[1] wrote Joseph Smith in describing public antipathy during the 1830s. "So embittered was the public mind against the truth that the press universally had been arrayed against us."[2] From the beginning the Mormons were sensitive to the opinions others held of them; for from these opinions, many of which were hostile, stemmed actions ranging from verbal abuse to pogroms.

The press influenced the public mind not only through the printed word, but through highly accessible mass-produced illustrations. Using wood, metal plates, or stone, prints were produced that contributed significantly to the popular image of Mormonism. The practice of engraving on wood or metal had been well established in colonial and early national America. Now, coincident with the birth of Mormonism, lithography was coming into its own.[3] At the same time, Andrew Jackson's flamboyant personality stimulated a sharp increase in caricature and cartoons.[4] At first artistic impressions of Mormons failed to keep pace with verbal images, but by the middle of the century, and continuing for at least sixty years, prints served as a barometer for the popular image of Mormonism.

Between 1830 and 1869 there were three phases in the development of the graphic depiction of Mormonism. The first period extended from the organization of the church to the mid-century mark. Many stereotypes evolved during this stage, though most appeared in written rather than illustrative form.[5] The few early illustrations were circulated almost exclusively through the medium of the illustrated anti-Mormon book.[6] The dominant images were that of the fraudulent prophet Joseph Smith, who appeared in almost every print, and benighted religious organi-

---

1. Joseph Smith, Jr., *History of the Church of Jesus Christ of Latter-day Saints*, 7 vols. (Salt Lake City: Deseret Book Co., 1960), 1:158.

2. Ibid., 1:273.

3. John and Katherine Ebert, *Old American Prints for Collectors* (New York: Charles Scribner's Sons, 1974), pp. 28–31.

4. William Murrell, *A History of American Graphic Humor, 1747–1865*, 2 vols. (New York: Cooper Square Publishers, Inc., 1967), 1:x.

5. For evidence of the wide range and vigor of these early images see John C. Bennett, *The History of the Saints* (Boston: Leland and Whiting, 1842). Stereotypes of subversive, dishonest, lustful, aggressive, autocratic, and economically and politically exploitative Mormons were there as well as the image of the victimized women. Moreover, the methods of guilt by association were also prevalent in the Bennett book.

6. An exception was the appearance of a previously published print in the *Anti-Mormon Almanac for 1842* (New York: [1841]).

zation. But like the Jewish image, which was built upon a foundation of religious difference and generalized later to economic, political, and other stereotypes, the anti-Mormon image was ready to be expanded.

From about 1850 to the Civil War Mormonism attracted national attention. Illustrations were a major means of expressing opinions about the religion. Prints multiplied rapidly. Mormons appeared in book illustrations as a plethora of competing novels, exposés, and historical works were rushed into print.[7] But it was the illustrated periodical enjoying its first blush of popularity that especially contributed to national pictorial image making. Now cartoons stood beside the sobering images from anti-Mormon books. Replacing the image of the fraudulent prophet in popularity, though that image continued, were images of polygamy, theocratic governance, and event-related subjects such as the Utah War. While Brigham Young became a focal point, with his rotund figure, bearded face, and independent manner inviting caricature, the central target was Mormonism.[8]

The chilling effects of the Civil War dampened the national ardor to do something about Mormon question. By comparison with the ferment of the decade preceding the war, the third phase—1861–69—was more restrained. With one or two exceptions, prints literally disappeared from the national magazines, but the intermittent publication of illustrated books reminded the Mormons they were not entirely displaced from national awareness.

The Early Years, 1830–50

During the first two decades of the church's existence, several factors limited its national exposure through the print media. The religious movement was not large and did not always seem newsworthy from a national viewpoint. Newspapers either ignored the Mormons or satisfied themselves with a few lines on the subject. Joseph Smith's campaign for the national presidency in 1844 probably would have stimulated some cartoons had it not been so early and abruptly terminated by his murder.[9] Located on the frontier for the most part, the Mormons were

7. Separately published prints by Currier and Ives and others also contributed to the popular image.

8. For broad outlines describing the nature of nineteenth-century American humor, see Constance Rourke, *American Humor: A Study of the National Character* (New York: Harcourt Brace Javanovich, 1971).

9. We have located cartoons of the other candidates in the 1844 election, but none of Joseph Smith; however, these early prints are not always easy to find.

removed from the centers of engraving on the East Coast.[10] Before the middle of the nineteenth century, almanacs, book illustrations, and separately published prints were the primary avenues of print production;[11] this meant limited media outlets and a narrow selection of topics. For these reasons any comparative analysis of cartoonists' and print makers' subjects of the 1830s and 1840s would show the Mormons most conspicuous by their absence.[12]

And yet there were a few visual representations of the new religious movement produced during those first two decades. Most images appeared in illustrated and anti-Mormon books, some of which were written by embittered ex-Mormons.[13] Two woodcuts in Eber D. Howe's *Mormonism Unvailed*, published in 1834, marked the debut of the pictorial representation of Mormonism.[14] The cuts were based on outlandish stories attributed in the text to the Smith family. In the first cut (Fig. 1) two stories were combined. One story asserted that a toad, hiding in the hillside repository of the plates that contained the ancient religious record of Mormon, was transformed into a devil which proceeded to assault the young Joseph. A variant account described Joseph Smith running from Satan with the plates, finally being overtaken, and the devil's kick lifting "him three or four feet from the ground."

The tale illustrated in the second cut (Fig. 2)[15] was based on

Fig. 1. Woodcut from Eber D. Howe's *Mormonism Unvailed* published in 1834.

Fig. 2. Woodcut from Eber D. Howe's *Mormonism Unvailed* published in 1834.

10. In addition to the distance factor, the costs of engraving on metal plates in the 1830s limited the number of prints. Frank L. Mott, *A History of American Magazines, 1741–1850*, 5 vols. (Cambridge, Mass.: Harvard University Press, 1957), 1:519. "In 1800 there were thirty-five engravers working in Philadelphia but only fourteen in New York City. Twenty years later Philadelphia increased the lead with sixty-three to only twenty-four for New York City." Ebert and Ebert, *Old American Prints*, p. 28.

11. We have searched through hundreds of almanacs at the American Antiquarian Society in Worcester, Mass., and the Library of Congress for the period 1820–75 without turning up much significant Mormon-related material, especially in graphics. For a helpful source on almanacs see Milton Drake, *Almanacs of the United States* (New York: The Scarecrow Press, 1962).

12. Gary L. Bunker and Davis Bitton, "Mormonism Veiled: Establishing the Visual Stereotype, 1830–1850" (unpublished paper in possession of the authors), examines some of the sympathetic images fostered by persecution.

13. Among those books published before 1850 that were adversely influenced by ex-Mormons were: Eber D. Howe, *Mormonism Unvailed* (Painesville, Ohio, 1834); Bennett, *History of the Saints; An Authentic History of Remarkable Persons* (New York: Wilson and Co., Brother Jonathon Press, 1848); and I. M'Gee, Van Dusen and Maria Van Dusen [Van Deusen], *Startling Disclosures of the Great Mormon Conspiracy Against the Liberties of This Country* . . . (New York: Blake and Jackson, 1849).

14. Howe, *Mormonism Unvailed*, frontispiece. The first cut also appeared in Origen Bacheler, *Mormonism Exposed* (New York, 1838) and the *Anti-Mormon Alamanac for 1842*.

15. For the textual descriptions, see Howe, *Mormonism Unvailed*, pp. 275–77.

something Joseph Smith allegedly told Joseph Knight, who told apostate Philastus Hurlbut, who reported the incident to Eber D. Howe. After burying the plates in a mountain, this story goes, Joseph Smith meets an aged gentleman carrying a monkey in a box. The prophet declines an offer to view the monkey for a small fee. Later, when Joseph ponders the strange interview, he is led to the Lord to inquire about the meaning of the experience. Too late he learns that the old man was none other than the angel Moroni and that if he had only paid for a glimpse of the monkey he would have been allowed to regain the plates.

The Howe cuts did not escape Joseph Smith's notice. He saw them as evidence of "redoubled fury by the enemy of righteousness, with his pitchfork of lies." Yet confident that Mormonism, "an impenetrable, immovable rock in the midst of the mighty deep," could absorb "the mountain waves of opposition," the prophet challenged Howe to continue his mischief "that the people may more readily discern between the righteous and the wicked."[16] No other prints of Mormonism have been found for the 1830s except for Origen Bacheler's use of one of Howe's cuts in his 1838 anti-Mormon publication. The only visual portrayals of the events of Mormonism's crowded first decade, therefore, came by way of restrospective flashbacks by printmakers after 1850.[17] Until the early 1840s written and word-of-mouth portrayals expressed the main public impressions of Mormonism.

Soon after their arrival as refugees in Illinois in 1839 and the establishment of a city, Nauvoo, on the Mississippi River, the Mormons were subjected to renewed assaults in the media. The first illustrations in the new decade appeared in John C. Bennett's serialized exposé in the *Sangamo Journal* during the summer of 1842. The exposé was published as a book in the fall of that year.[18] Bitter after his excommunication, Bennett referred to Nauvoo as the "Mother of Harlots" and the church as the "Mormon monster." He wished "to appeal to the feelings and fears of the Christian community."

F. E. Worcester prepared three wood engravings reflecting Bennett's angry mood.[19] Each described an allegedly secret Mormon organization in diabolical action: the "Daughter of Zion," the "Destroying Angels," and the "Order Lodge."[20] The Destroy-

16. Smith, *History of the Church*, 2:268.

17. See Bunker and Bitton, "Mormonism Veiled."

18. Bennett, *History of the Saints*.

19. Fernando E. Worcester, the wood engraver, "was active in Boston from about 1836 to 1853 and was connected with the firms of Brown and Worcester (1846–47) and Worcester and Pierce (1851–52)." George C. Groce and David H. Wallace, *The New-York Historical Society's Dictionary of Artists in America, 1564–1860* (New Haven: Yale University Press, 1957), p. 702.

20. Bennett, *History of the Saints*, pp. 263, 269, 273.

ing Angels were twelve men who, according to Bennett, were drawn from the elite of the Daughter of Zion organization. Curiously, when they executed any important decree they were always arrayed in "female attire." "They also pledge themselves to poison the wells and the food and drink of dissenters, apostates, and all enemies of Zion, and to murder those who refuse to tithe...."[21]

Initially Mormon leadership responded to Bennett's inflammatory rhetoric by maintaining a relatively low profile. "We shall content ourselves with answering his falsehoods and misrepresentations without giving publicity to them," stated an editorial in the *Times and Seasons*.[22] As evidence mounted that the *New York Herald* "had been influenced by the misrepresentation," Joseph Smith wrote a parable using animal symbols reproving some representatives of the media.[23] Joseph Smith suggested that James Gordon Bennett, editor of the *New York Herald*, repeated the brayings of an ass. "Even thou hast condescended to degrade thyself by uniting with the basest of animals," chided the Mormon prophet. Of course, the parable did not silence press critics.

The Reverend Henry Caswall, professor of divinity at Kemper College in Missouri, joined the ranks of anti-Mormon authors.[24] Caswall's penchant for art led him to sketch the only illustration in the book. Prepared for printing by an English lithographer, the frontispiece depicted an incident in which Joseph Smith was presented a Greek manuscript of the Psalms, which he supposedly identified as a dictionary of Egyptian hieroglyphics (Fig. 3). "Them figures is Egyptian hieroglyphics, and them which follows is the interpretation of the hieroglyphics, written in the reformed Egyptian language," said Joseph Smith as quoted by Caswall. "Them characters is like the letters that was engraved on the golden plates."[25] Impugning Joseph Smith by putting ungrammatical expressions in his mouth may have undermined Caswall's scholarly credibility, but like other inaccurate accounts, it also helped establish a negative image of the Mormons.[26]

The events leading to the martyrdom of Joseph Smith and the expulsion of the Mormons from Nauvoo did not generate

---

21. Ibid., p. 271.

22. Smith, *History of the Church*, 5:79.

23. Ibid., 5:274–77.

24. Henry Caswall, *The Prophet of the Nineteenth Century* (London: J. G. F. and J. Rivington, 1843). The lithograph appears to have been made by Picken, an employee of Day and Haghe, Lithographers to the Queen.

25. Caswall, *The Prophet of the Nineteenth Century*, p. 223.

26. For a discussion of Caswall see Hugh Nibley, *The Myth Makers* (Salt Lake City: Bookcraft, 1961), pp. 191–288.

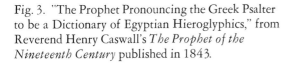

Fig. 3. "The Prophet Pronouncing the Greek Psalter to be a Dictionary of Egyptian Hieroglyphics," from Reverend Henry Caswall's *The Prophet of the Nineteenth Century* published in 1843.

sympathetic prints; however, some illustrations appeared that were at least neutral.[27] Sidney Roberts' *Great Distress and Loss of American Citizens* (1848) publicized the plight of the Mormons.[28] Two prints decorated the volume. One, entitled "A Partial View of the Massacre of the Mormons," was borrowed from a pre-Revolutionary War representation of the Boston Massacre (Fig. 4).[29] For those few readers who may have recognized the print, associating the Boston Massacre with the massacre of Mormons probably did not hurt the public image of Mormonism. The other engraving from Roberts shows "Mormons leaving the city of Nauvoo, February 1st, 1846."[30]

Even as the Mormons were straggling across the plains to make their initial settlements in the Great Basin, two works produced or influenced by disaffected Mormons added to the negative visual image. One entitled *An Authentic History of Remarkable Persons* claimed that Joseph Smith set a woman's hen house on fire, "poisoned the house dog . . . , introduced . . . medicine into the coffee pot . . . , [and] spent two years in Massachusetts prison under an assumed name for horse steal-

27. Paul D. Ellsworth, "Mobocracy and the Rule of Law: American Press Reaction to the Murder of Joseph Smith," *BYU Studies* 20 (Fall 1979):71–82.

28. Sidney Roberts, *Great Distress and Loss of Lives of American Citizens* (Iowa City: 1848). An entry in Smith's *History of the Church* on 4 December 1840 notes that an Elder Sidney Roberts was excommunicated (4:237). If this is the same Sidney Roberts, his loss of membership evidently produced little bitterness as contrasted with John C. Bennett and others.

29. Roberts, *Great Distress*, back cover. This print is one of the variants of the famous Henry Pelham engraving which Paul Revere apparently copied and sold. For a history of engravings of the Boston Massacre see Clarence S. Brigham, *Paul Revere's Engravings* (New York: Atheneum, 1969). This engraving differs slightly in detail from each of the plates appearing in the Brigham book.

30. Roberts, *Great Distress*, p. 13. The name Lines appears in the lower right-hand corner of the print. The photograph of the print was obtained from the Beinicke Library at Yale University.

Fig. 4. "A Partial View of the Massacre of the Mormons," from Sidney Roberts' *Great Distress and Loss of Lives of American Citizens* published in 1848.

ing."[31] *An Authentic History of Remarkable Persons* mocked several Mormon temple ordinances on the basis of information from a "seceding Mormon named Thomas White." An absurdly dressed, bespectacled, wiry-haired Joseph Smith, obviously drawn by an artist either unfamiliar with or not caring about Smith's actual appearance, was shown in the Nauvoo temple (Fig. 5).[32]

Also taking advantage of public interest in the temple ceremonies were ex-Mormons Maria and Increase Van Deusen, whose book went through twenty-three editions from 1847 to 1864.[33] The titles, illustrations, and even the text varied depending upon the publisher and the motivation to stimulate sales. The illustrations, complementing the emotional tone of the text,[34] included a caricature of the Council of the Twelve Apostles suggestively captioned "Brigham Young's Twelve Apostles (Imposters) concocting their great schemes of Deviltry

---

31. *Remarkable Persons*, facing p. 8.

32. Ibid., p. 4.

33. Chad Flake, ed., *A Mormon Bibliography, 1830–1930* (Salt Lake City: University of Utah Press, 1978).

34. Some illustrations in the Van Deusen series as well as elsewhere refute Rudolf Glanz' contention that "There is not to be found among all the Mormon caricatures a real erotic drawing. . . ." Rudolf Glanz, *The Jew in Early American Wit and Graphic Humor* (New York: KTAV Publishing House, Inc., 1973), pp. 20–21. It should also be mentioned that some of the Van Deusen editions were not illustrated.

Fig. 5. "Initiation of the First Degree," from *An Authentic History of Remarkable Persons* published in 1848.

in California, Spiritual Wife System, &c,"[35] a detailed foldout illustration, and even color plates. With the publication of several of the Van Deusen editions by the mid-century point, the first phase of the pictorial representation of Mormonism came to a close.

Clearly, it was the negative image that was most powerful and persistent during these early years. Those who derived their impression of the movement from illustrations alone or from illustrations complementing verbal descriptions could scarcely help but see Mormonism as a combination of stupidity, superstition, secrecy, sinister ceremonies, militarism, and tyrannical exploitation. This image, as historian David Brion Davis has demonstrated, was similar to popular stereotypes of Catholics and Masons and told more about public fears and obsessions than about these movements.[36] In any case, the negative stereotype that shaped attitudes and even official policies did not arise for the first time in the Great Basin; it was an integral part of Mormon experience from the beginning.

The Mormon Image at Mid–Century, 1850–69

If the first two decades of Mormonism provided the seedbed for artistic imagery, the 1850s saw the sprouting, rooting, and maturing of the plant. By the Civil War, both textual and pictorial depictions of the Mormons had firmly established the national stereotypes. There would be later embellishments and elaborations as new events transpired, but these would be variations on themes laid down during or before the antebellum period.

Three important factors combined to fix the negative stereotype of Mormonism. First, the social climate in the United States permitted, even encouraged with impunity, open hostility to unpopular ethnic, racial, and religious groups. Second, several incidents in Utah territory in the 1850s stimulated resentment: the public avowal of polygamy; clashes between Mormon leaders and U.S. officials that led to federal judges leaving Utah and charging that it was a dictatorial theocracy; the Utah War of 1857–58 that reiterated these same charges and increased national awareness of the question; and, finally, the Mountain

---

35. I. M'Gee Van Dusen and Maria Van Dusen [Van Deusen], *Startling Disclosures of the Mormon Spiritual Wife System . . .* (New York: 1864), facing p. 10.

36. David Brion Davis, "Some Themes of Counter-Subversion: An Analysis of Anti-Masonic, Anti-Catholic, and Anti-Mormon Literature," *The Mississippi Valley Historical Review* 47 (September 1960):205–24; John Higham, *Strangers in the Land* (New York: Atheneum, 1975), preface to 2d ed. We are aware that prejudice is determined by many causes. Space does not permit us to discuss the complex determinants, but the brief statement in the text is intended to refer to that complexity.

Meadows Massacre. All these provided material for the development of a stereotype of Mormonism.[37]

The third development in the establishment of the Mormon stereotype was the emergence and proliferation of the illustrated periodical. "The illustration mania is upon our people," observed the *Cosmopolitan Art Journal* in 1857. "Nothing but illustrated works are profitable to publishers; while the illustrated magazines and newspapers are vastly popular."[38] *The Lantern, Yankee Notions, Frank Leslie's Illustrated Weekly Newspaper, Frank Leslie's Budget of Fun, Harper's Weekly, Vanity Fair, The Old Soldier, Phunny Phellow, The Picayune,* and *Nick Nax* all began publication during or just before the 1850s. And all displayed Mormonism both textually and pictorially.[39] While visual representations had been disseminated by books, pamphlets, broadsides, almanacs, and separately published prints, none of these had as much power to shape popular attitudes as the illustrated periodical. At the outset of the Civil War both *Harper's* and *Leslie's* weeklies exceeded the 100,000 circulation mark, and the monthly *Yankee Notions* sold 150,000 copies as early as 1858.[40] In these publications words and pictures worked together to produce the stereotype.

When federally appointed judges Brocchus and Brandebury left Utah in 1851 and returned to Washington, they charged that the Mormons were disloyal to the United States, that they were practicing polygamy, and that Brigham Young had been guilty of malfeasance as governor. Pro and con discussions of these charges included a highly critical editorial in the *St. Louis Republican* accusing the judges of abandoning their posts.[41] *The Lantern,* an illustrated weekly, offered a satirical account on 17 January 1852:

> Judges are not recognized in the Scriptures of Utah—especially United States Judges, two of whom have been compelled to make their exodus to the Atlantic Slope. Their feet were beautiful upon

---

37. See Introduction, note 6.

38. Mott, *History of Magazines,* 2:192.

39. "*Yankee Doodle* and *John Donkey* eked out brief careers at the end of the forties, *The Lantern* threw its glimmer over Millard Fillmore's last two years in the White House, and *Yankee Notions* held out from 1852 into the seventies. But the first magazine to establish itself firmly in political caricature was *Harper's Weekly,* founded in 1857. Then in the fateful months of John Brown's raid, December 1859, *Vanity Fair* appeared. . . ." Allan Nevins and Frank Weitenkampf, *A Century of Political Cartoons* (New York: Scribners, 1944), p. 13. The dates of the other publications were: *The Picayune,* 1847–60; *The Old Soldier,* January–June 1852; *Nick Nax* 1857–75; *Frank Leslie's Budget of Fun,* 1859–78; *Frank Leslie's Illustrated Newspaper,* 1855–1922; *Phunny Phellow,* 1859–76.

40. Mott, *History of Magazines,* 2:10, 182.

41. B. H. Roberts, *A Comprehensive History of the Church of Jesus Christ of Latter-day Saints,* 6 vols. (Provo, Utah: Brigham Young University Press, 1957), 3:535–37.

Fig. 6. "Mormon Breastworks and U.S. Troops. *Officer U.S.A.*: 'Trumpeter! Sound the retreat! We never can carry that Battery in the world. Cesar himself would be defeated before such Breastworks.' " *The Old Soldier*, 1 April 1852.

the mountains, for they journeyed briskly. And the twain have writ a chronicle, and the chronicle is true. Their record saith there is no division in the Mormon Church, but rather multiplication. The High Priest, even Brigham, hath forty wives spiritual, and all the forty are under twenty-five. . . . And there be other Saints, whose matrimonial crops are plentious and heavy in the cradle of the husbandman; for Utah is not a barren land. . . . Now the Prophet Young, whose given name is Brigham, denieth the authority of this Nation, and goeth for the "solidarity" of the Mormon peoples and opposeth intervention. And lest the righteous be tempted with the public silver and gold, he seizeth and putteth it away privily, where no man can find it. And the Saints are satisfied with the Prophet and mourn not the loss. All these things, and more also, are writ in the Chronicles of the Judges, who tarried awhile in the Land.

Before the outset of the Utah War in 1857, even before the public acknowledgment of polygamy in 1852, polygamy and hostility to the United States were being linked together in portrayals of the Mormons.

A lithograph published in the 1 April 1852 issue of *The Old Soldier* employed double entendre to exploit the twin themes of polygamy and Mormon defiance (Fig. 6).[42] A brief textual commentary supplemented the caption.

Nothing short of disgrace, disaster, and defeat can await the United States troops, should they be reckless enough to attack the Mormons of Deseret in their formidable entrenchments. Protected by such "Breastworks" they may safely banish fear, while with their Light

42. A note in the file at the American Antiquarian Society, Worcester, Mass., by the late director of the Society, Clarence S. Brigham, suggests: "This set of lithographs in *The Old Soldier* was published in 1852 at 69 Nassau Street, New York. John L. Magee was listed as a lithographer at 69 Nassau Street, in New York Business Directory for 1852–53. He executed similar lithographs. It has been thought that these lithographs were by David C. Johnston, but in no way are they like his work, and he was in Boston in 1852."

Artillery they can raise such a noise about the ears of their enemies that neither tactics nor discipline for a moment can withstand. Total annihilation must inevitably result.

The simple reversal of sexual roles subtly maligned both Mormon men and women. Moreover, the early pictorial views of Mormon children presaged the development of special stereotypes for youthful Mormons. Perhaps the most remarkable thing about this lithograph is the way it anticipated the Utah War and provided a humorous situation that would be exploited later on.

Most of the illustrations published between 1852 and 1856 focused on polygamy. Some of them were relatively innocuous. For example, Thomas Butler Gun, a cartoonist for *The Lantern*, had Brigham Young exclaim to Horace Greeley, "Say, Brother Greeley, have you got the Mormon Life of Scott fixed yet? If yer have, I guess I'll take a thousand, as I should like to give a copy to each of my wives!"[43] About the same time a separately published print over the caption "The Follies of the Age, Vive La Humbug!!" showed an oxcart full of Mormon women labeled "Salt Lake, Brigham Young."[44] In July 1854 *Yankee Notions'* first cartoon on Mormonism depicted the "fashionable arrival" of "Mr. Pratt, M. C. from Utah, twenty wives and seventy-five children." Just two years later the same periodical began the use of pejorative animal symbolism with a sketch of a rooster surrounded by hens and captioned "A foul (fowl) piece of Mormonism."[45] Polygamy could thus be hinted at while suggesting at the same time that Mormons were less than human.[46]

While most illustrated books on Mormons from 1850 to the Civil War were merciless in their treatment of Mormonism, Charles Mackay aspired to represent the faith with detachment.[47] He concentrated on a history of early Mormon events to 1850. (Since his book preceded the announcement of polygamy and the disenchanted murmuring of federal officials in Utah, objectivity may have been easier.) He collected "rude sketches, or

43. *The Lantern*, 18 September 1852. The caption alluded to the common practice of the day for newspapers to print inexpensive books written by Sir Walter Scott and others. See Russell Nye, *The Unembarrassed Muse* (New York: Dial Press, 1970), p. 25.

44. This print is in the graphics collection of the American Antiquarian Society.

45. *Yankee Notions*, May 1856.

46. A Danish anti-Mormon tract in 1857 represented Mormons with a picture of a guinea baboon. See Jergen W. Schmidt, *Oh, Du Zion I Vest* (Kobenhavn: Rosenkilde og Bagger, 1965), plate after 144. On animal symbolism, see Leonard J. Arrington and Davis Bitton, *The Mormon Experience* (New York: Knopf, 1979), pp. 60–61.

47. Charles Mackay, *The Mormons or Latter-day Saints* (London: Office of the National Illustrated Library, 1851). See Leonard J. Arrington, "Charles Mackay and His 'True and Impartial History' of the Mormons," *Utah Historical Quarterly* 36 (Winter 1968):24–40.

minute descriptions, of persons to whom the spots were familiar, and who were, in many cases, eyewitnesses of the incidents depicted." He borrowed portraits and scenes of Mormons performing ordinances from the artist Frederick Piercy. "Other subjects," he said, "have been copied from prints published under the sanction of the sect." Engravings from Mackay's work were reproduced again and again in subsequent books and articles on Mormonism, but the textual context did not always remain as neutral as Mackay's.

Far more characteristic of the mood of book illustrations during this era of anti-Mormon agitation were prints from Maria Ward's *Female Life Among the Mormons*, Orvilla S. Belisle's *The Prophets: Or Mormonism Unveiled*, and Alfreda Eva Bell's *Boadicea, The Mormon Wife: Life–Scenes in Utah*. Popular fiction in the 1850s was dominated by women. " 'America,' Hawthorne wrote angrily, 'is now wholly given over to a damned mob of scribbling women.' "[48] Although panned by a book review in the *London Times* as "altogether apocryphal" and "the latest Yankee hoax," Maria Ward's fictional piece, for example, sold enough copies in America to whet the appetite of the foreign book market, where French, German, and Swedish translations satisfied popular tastes.[49] Helping to sell these books were such prints as "Lizzie Monroe in Her Prison—Brigham Young Making Insulting Proposals,"[50] or "Jeannette Is Gagged and Carried Away."[51]

When misunderstandings between the Mormons and the federal government led to General Albert Sidney Johnston being sent to Utah territory with an army, Brigham Young insisted on his rights as governor and prepared to resist. The result was the short-lived Utah War, consisting mainly of harassment of the advancing federal troops by Mormon guerrillas, a delay of the army, a threat of Mormon evacuation of their Utah settlements (partially carried out by the Big Move), and eventual settlement and reconciliation.[52] This campaign provided subject matter for the national periodicals during much of 1857 and 1858.

The Buchanan administration did not escape ridicule for this

48. Nye, *The Unembarrassed Muse*, p. 22. Naturally, women had no corner on the anti-Mormon book market; illustrated books by men were equally destructive. For example, John Hyde, *Mormonism: Its Leaders and Designs* (New York: W. P. Fetridge & Co., 1857); Robert Richards [pseud.], *The California Cruso* (New York: Stanford and Swords, 1854).

49. Flake, *A Mormon Bibliography*, pp. 756–58.

50. Orvilla Belisle, *The Prophets of Mormonism Unveiled* (Philadelphia: Wm. White Smith, 1855), frontispiece.

51. Alfreda Eva Bell, ed., *Boadicea: The Mormon Wife* (Baltimore: Arthur R. Orton, 1855), p. 83.

52. On the Utah War see James B. Allen and Glen M. Leonard, *The Story of the Latter-day Saints* (Salt Lake City: Deseret Book Company, 1976), ch. 9 and supporting bibliography.

Fig. 7. "Brigham Young from behind His Breastworks Charging the United States Troops." Privately printed and offered for sale at 217 Walnut Street, Philadelphia.

needless expenditure of energy and funds. But for the Mormons, the war brought them repeatedly to public attention where they were ridiculed as polygamists and traitors. A Philadelphia lithographer seized the opportunity and offered for sale an illustration of fine detail and flagged captions that was essentially a restatement of the earlier "Breastworks" idea (Fig. 7).[53] The theme had received an added boost from Mormon leader Heber C. Kimball's 1857 tongue-in-cheek remark; "I have wives enough to whip out the United States . . ."[54]

By this time two of the new illustrated weeklies—*Leslie's Illustrated Weekly* and *Harper's Weekly*—had surpassed their rivals. They more than any of the others established the illustrated weekly as a fixture of American media. Both of these periodicals showed great interest in the Mormons and the Utah War.

---

53. The curator of graphic arts at the American Antiquarian Society, Worcester Mass., did not know the source of the print except that it was "for sale at 217 Walnut Street, Philadelphia." The estimated date given to the lithograph is 1857.

54. Heber C. Kimball in *The Journal of Discourses* 26 vols. (Liverpool, Engl.: Albert Carrington, 1854–86), 5:95, 250, sermons delivered 26 July 1857 and 20 September 1857.

Fig. 8. "Brigham Young's Preparations for the Defence of Utah—The Result." *Frank Leslie's Illustrated Newspaper*, 19 December 1857.

Fig. 9. "Flight of Brigham Young, from a Drawing Done Here on the Spot by Our Own Clairvoyant Artist." *Frank Leslie's Illustrated Newspaper*, 5 June 1858.

The first Mormon cartoon appeared in *Frank Leslie's Illustrated Newspaper* 19 December 1857 (Fig. 8). It was a serial cartoon, which anticipated the comic strip of a later period, and it contained the popular theme of a female Mormon militia but with a new twist: the fickle female troops lose combat readiness the minute the dashing gentile appears. With Mormon men unable to match the allurements of their gentile counterparts, the Utah War comes to an end.

Six months after the appearance of this serial cartoon, an artist for *Leslie's*, Justin H. Howard, sketched another imagined resolution of the war on 5 June 1858 (Figs. 9–11). Soldiers from Johnston's Army were hiding under the huge hoopskirts of the Mormon women, who, according to the caption, "Make an Amicable Settlement of All Their Difficulties." Another cartoon by Howard on the same page parodied Brigham Young, complete with balloon caption, fleeing "from the wrath to come." It was the image of a cowardly leader apparently leaving his wives and children to fend for themselves.

In the meantime *Harper's Weekly* was offering its own satirical version of the United States' invasion of Mormon Utah. The first Mormon cartoon was published in *Harper's Weekly* on 28 November 1857. It appropriated the familiar theme of Mormon males mustering female recruits. A much more imaginative set of cartoons introduced comic figures.[55] Brigham Young's public image was not enhanced by caricaturing him as the dull, piggish caretaker of Brigadier General Bombshell's bevy of wives. And like *Leslie's*, *Harper's* gave its satiric version of the consummation of the war (Fig. 12).[56] The shackled Mormon men were obliged to watch as their consorts catered to their beguiling captors. There was a mixture of condescension

Fig. 10. "The Mormon Ladies Make an Amicable Settlement of All Their Difficulties." *Frank Leslie's Illustrated Newspaper*, 5 June 1858.

Fig. 11. "The Mormons Convert Their Carts into Moveable Harems, and Go on Their Way Rejoicing." *Frank Leslie's Illustrated Newspaper*, 5 June 1858.

55. *Harper's Weekly*, 1 May 1858.
56. Ibid., 22 May 1858.

Fig. 12. "Frightful Scene of Carnage and Desolation at the Sack of Salt Lake City by the United States Troops." *Harper's Weekly*, 22 May 1858.

and self-congratulation inherent in the theme of the "dashing gentile."

Of all the illustrated weeklies of the 1850s none surpassed *Harper's Weekly* in space given to the Mormons. The following sampling of news dispatches demonstrates *Harper's* negative editorial stance regarding the Mormons.

> *February 21, 1857.* In regard to the Mormon children, they appear like a neglected uncared-for set, generally dirty and ill-clad. The majority of them are girls, and this troubles the women very much, for they know a female is doomed to slavery and a life of misery. . . . These children are suffered to grow up in ignorance and vice. Without the hallowed influence of home to restrain them, they are vicious, profane and obscene.

> *May 23, 1857.* The Bishop of Provo, a creature named Carter, officiated at the funeral of Nash, and after concluding the prayer over the dead body of the father, turned to the weeping girl, informed her that she was now unprotected, and must become his wife! In less than ten days she was forced to yield, and now swells the number of Carter's "spirituals" to seven.

However, the illustrations in *Harper's Weekly* were more benign. On 10 October 1857, three illustrations showed Brigham Young's family going to church, in their family parlor, and at a family dinner. A fourth panel was a view of a Mormon dance with a high ratio of females to males. But the title, "Scenes in an American Harem," was sufficiently titillating to make up for any lack of excitement in the pictures themselves. Most of the additional thirteen pictorial representations were engravings taken from the photographs of David H. Burr, the surveyor-general of Utah territory and the deputy surveyor, a Mr. Mogo.[57] There was nothing sensational about the engrav-

57. The experiences of Burr and Mogo in Utah may have contributed more to the image of Mormonism than their rather mundane photographs. They reported being harassed severely by Mormons. See *Harper's Weekly*

ings—mostly selected scenes in Salt Lake City—but the accompanying text managed to convey invidious connotations. For example, "The Calaboose in Salt Lake City" was described as the place where gentiles were incarcerated whose "crime was that of being American citizens."[58] The residence of Heber C. Kimball, "the most vulgar and profane man in the Mormon Church," was matter-of-factly shown with this commentary: "His 'spirituals' frequently run away from him, and when at home quarrel so much that he finds several buildings absolutely necessary. Our view of his group of dwellings is the best evidence of the fact."[59]

Joining the chorus of visual and textual commentators were two other publications—*Nick Nax* and *The Picayune.* Each was more interested in news making than news reporting. Entertainment, not accuracy, was their goal. Riddles, jokes, light verse, and comic illustrations captured the fancy of indiscriminate readers.

The prizewinning riddle sent in by one of the subscribers of *Nick Nax* during the Utah War went something like this: "Why is it probable that the Mormons will, at an early day, be recognized as Saints by the whole United States? Because they will soon be *cannonized* by order of the Government."[60] A few months later a full-page serial cartoon entitled "The Mormon War" offered several stereotypes (Fig. 13)[61]—contrasting the "Mormon Rooster" with the "American Eagle," linking blacks and Mormons, indicting Mormon males as cowards, and poking fun at Mormon women, children, and Brigham Young. "The Mormon Love Song," a parody on polygamy, appeared in the July 1858 issue of *Nick Nax.* It satirically pours forth versified stereotypes of the insensitive husband and exploited wife.

Mormonism fared no better in the pages of *The Picayune.* Frank Bellew, one of the most popular cartoonists of his time, managed to attack Horace Greeley and ridicule Mormonism at the same time. The accompanying text explained the cartoon.

> Such a man as...Horace Greeley, who ever goes on in his...blundering way, reminds us always of the b'hoy who said, "If I don't have a muss I shall spile." Greeley must have an ism or he'll "spile." Having *Faith* large (we speak phrenologically), with firmness and the perceptives small, he generally goes in favor of anything new which may turn up. But in certain cases . . . he is found in the opposition. . . .

---

1 (31 October 1857): 694. For more detailed descriptions of relations between the two surveyors and the Mormons see: Gustive O. Larson, *The "Americanization" of Utah for Statehood* (San Marino, Calif.: The Huntington Library, 1971), p. 14, and Nels Anderson, *Desert Saints* (Chicago: University of Chicago Press, 1966), pp. 149–52.

58. *Harper's Weekly,* 6 November 1858.

59. Ibid., 18 September 1858.

60. *Nick Nax,* February 1858.

61. Ibid., June 1858.

THE MORMON LOVE SONG

Say, Susan wilt thou come with me
    In sweet community to live?
Of heart, and hand, and home, to thee
    A sixteenth part I freely give
Of all the love that swells my breast,
    Of all the honor of my name,
Of worldly wealth by me possessed,
    A sixteenth portion thou shalt claim.
Nay, tell me not too many share
    The blessings that I offer thee;
Thou'lt find but fifteen others there,
    A household happy, gay and free.
A moderate household, I may say;
    My neighbor has as many more,
And brother Brigham o'er the way
    Luxuriates in forty-four.
I promise thee a life of ease,
    And for thyself I'll let thee choose
Such duties as thy fancy please;
    Say, Susan, canst thou still refuse?
Sephronia cooks and sweeps the floors,
    And Hepzibah makes up the beds,
Jemima answers all the doors,
    And Prudence combs the children's heads.
The household duties all develop
    On each according to her lot;
But from such labor I'll absolve
    My Susan, if she likes them not.
Into thy hands such tasks as take
    A dignity, will I consign;
I'll let thee black my boots, or make
    The sock and shirt department thine.
I'll give thee whatsoe'er thou wilt—
    So it be but a sixteenth part;
It would be the deepest depth of guilt
    To slight the rest who share my heart.
Then wilt thou not thy fraction yield
    To make up my domestic bliss?
Say yes—and let our joy be sealed
    With just the sixteenth of a kiss.

Fig. 13. "The Mormon War." *Nick Nax*, June 1858.

He is down on Mormonism, and when he comes down, he comes down like a brick church. . . . The picture represents the great Ismist wreaking his vengeance on the rural Mormons—the Polygamists of the farm yard.[62]

Bellew, anticipating doing the illustrations for "Ye piquante histories of ye Mormons," scheduled for publication in a future issue of the magazine, warmed up with a caricature of "Joe Smith, the founder of Roosterism, as now flourishing in Utah" (Fig. 14).[63] Although leadership had long since passed from Joseph Smith to Brigham Young, the founding Mormon prophet occasionally reappeared as a subject of the cartoonist's work.

When *Yankee Notions* printed "Ye Popular Idea of Brigham Young and His Followers" in April 1858 (Fig. 15), it demonstrated the power of pictorial symbols to convey a number of ideas. The goat caricature of Brigham Young was a symbol of lust. The horns of some of the prostrate followers, although not a new idea, were an early graphic representation of that image.[64] The enthusiasm of the females in the background, apparently for Brigham Young, was one of the many stereotypes of Mormon women. The unusual facial expressions underscored the presumed peculiarities of the adherents to this faith. The flag of liberty in the midst of the Mormons was a parody of the "indiscriminate allegiance" of the submissive followers.

A companion cartoon in the same issue of *Yankee Notions* presented another persistent theme.[65] The idea of a cooperative alliance and common destiny of Mormons and Indians was theologically grounded in the Book of Mormon. Suspicion of actual Mormon complicity with the Indians originated in the 1830s, but the possibility of alliance had been renewed with the Utah War. "God Almighty will arouse every tribe and every nation that exists in the East, West, North, and South," said Heber C. Kimball, "and they will be on hand for our relief."[66] The grotesque caricature of the Indians symbolized the contempt in which they were held. Linking the two unpopular groups in

Fig. 14. "Past Events Cast Their Shadows Behind. Joe Smith, the founder of Roosterism, as now flourishing in Utah." *The Picayune*, 12 September 1857.

Fig. 15. "Ye Popular Idea of Brigham Young and His Followers." *Yankee Notions*, April 1858.

62. *The Picayune*, 25 July 1857. The same cartoon with a slightly different caption appeared in *Phunny Phellow*, October 1859.

63. *The Picayune*, 12 September 1857, p. 120. Thus far we have been unable to find the illustrated history of the Mormons in the pages of *The Picayune*.

64. Cf. Karl E. Young, "Why Mormons Were Said to Wear Horns," in Thomas E. Cheney, ed., *Lore of Faith and Folly* (Salt Lake City: University of Utah Press, 1971), pp. 111–12. As early as 1842 General Wilson Law, in a conversation with Joseph Smith, had said, "Well, from reports, we had reason to think the Mormons were a peculiar people, different from other people, having horns or something of the kind; but I find they look like other people; indeed, I think Mr. Smith a very good looking man." Joseph Smith, *History of the Church*, 5:214.

65. See for background Lawrence G. Coates, "A History of Indian Education by the Mormons, 1830–1900" (Ph.D. dissertation, Ball State University, Muncie, Ind., 1969).

66. *Journal of Discourses*, 5:278.

the public mind exploited prejudices to malign both Indians and Mormons.

The Mountain Meadows Massacre of 1857, in which members of a wagon train from Arkansas were killed, kept the Mormon national reputation from improving. This unfortunate event was investigated as early as 1858. The present scholarly conclusion is that the local Mormon leaders in southern Utah were mainly responsible for the massacre, and Brigham Young did not know about the action until it was too late to stop it.[67] However, the mere fact that the incident occurred in the midst of the Mormons in sparsely settled Utah was enough to create a powerful negative symbol. On 13 August 1858, *Harper's Weekly* published a front-page exposé of the massacre with an accompanying sketch. Already thought of as strange and exotic because of plural marriage, the Mormons were also seen as stupid, dishonest pawns of a cruel and tyrannical prophet. All of these themes could be hinted at by mention or depiction of the Mountain Meadows Massacre, which, incidentally, appealed to the perennial human interest in violence. Of course, sweeping generalizations implied that the tragedy typified what one might expect from all Mormons. Furthermore, the prints and reports did not reflect the complexity of events or motivations leading up to the encounter. During the post-Civil War period, few subjects would be repeated more often in the visual portrayal of Mormonism.

To a certain degree, then, the singularity of Mormonism plus the unwise actions of some Mormons during the fifties were partially responsible for the public image. While the Mormons did in fact practice polygamy and a massacre did take place, and so on, selecting certain points, magnifying them, and taking them out of context for purposes of ridicule created a distorted view of the Mormons. The stereotypes were neither accurate nor fair. Blacks, Jews, Poles, Germans, Chinese, native Americans—any study of group stereotypes demonstrates the same point.[68] Our analysis of the image of the Mormons is thus a case study of a larger phenomenon.

Closing out the decade, *Harper's Weekly* reported with a sketch the notable Horace Greeley–Brigham Young interview, which was also satirized by the *New York Picayune*.[69] Other

---

67. On the massacre the standard treatment is Juanita Brooks, *The Mountain Meadows Massacre* (Norman: University of Oklahoma Press, 1950).

68. Gordon W. Allport, *The Nature of Prejudice* (Garden City, N. Y.: Doubleday Co., 1954).

69. The Horace Greeley-Brigham Young interview occurred on 15 July 1859. However, the content of the interview did not appear in *Harper's Weekly* until 3 September 1859. *The Picayune*, 27 August 1859, gave a satirical rendition of the experience.

Fig. 16. "The Republican Party Going to the Right House."
Lithograph published by Currier and Ives, 152 Nassau St., New York.

prints in 1859 and 1860 bordered on being sensational.[70] One print from the redoubtable firm of Currier and Ives included Mormons among the symbols intended to defeat Lincoln's bid for the presidency (Fig. 16).[71] Still another print in *Yankee Notions* in October of 1860 suggestively alluded to precocious sexuality in Mormon children. An illustration in the 11 February 1860 *Vanity Fair* depicted a subhuman, horned Brigham Young gesturing with one hand at a sign warning gentiles, the other hand firmly holding his "Pandean, polygam pipe" (Fig. 17). The illustrator's idea derived from a news account detailing Young's recent illness.

> The Mormon Hierarch has long been playing a game of "blind man's bluff" with the government of this country—a game in which we are sorry to think the government has allowed itself to be so utterly cornered that the muffler should, long since, have been conferred to Presidential features. But matters are now so bad at Polygamutah, that even Brig. Young himself declines, perhaps, to give his countenance openly to them, and, therefore, keeps the blinder on so as to be blind to what is going on about him. . . .

Fig. 17. "The Veiled Prophet of Polygamutah."
Vanity Fair, 11 February 1860.

70. A vicious misrepresentation of the Mormons appeared in *Harper's Weekly*, 26 February 1859, p. 132. Two prints showed a child being shot by Mormons for testifying against the "Danites."

71. This separately published print is in the graphic arts collection of the American Antiquarian Society, Worcester, Mass.

Fig. 18. Illustration from *Artemus Ward's Panorama* published in 1869.

It is high time for that Pan to be "brought over the coals." Territories are less savage when abandoned to their primitive bears and indigenous buffaloes than when subjected to the half-civilized influence of such a socialism as the Mormon megatherium: and we doubt if the Valley of the Lake of Salt, in the days when no footmarks fell on its crystal-frosted soil save those of the fierce beast of the mountain and plain, ever displayed, have [half] so beastly a sight as that of the grizzly goat-herd, Brigham, leading his hoofed and horned flock to the sound of his Pandean, Polygam pipe.[72]

The Image After the War

The third segment of the development of the public image of Mormonism covered the Civil War and Reconstruction period (1861–69). The coming of the Civil War diverted media attention away from Mormonism to some extent and illustrations on Mormon themes almost stopped.[73] A lone cartoon in *Frank Leslie's Budget of Fun* in the fall of 1865, using the timely war bonds issue as a springboard for mirth, facetiously displayed "Brigham Young's investment in the 7.30 interest bearing bonds" as seven wives and two infants thrown in as coupons, the babies presumably making up the fractional part of the interest.[74]

Artemus Ward's visit to Salt Lake City in 1864 inspired an illustrated lecture tour entitled "Artemus Ward among the Mormons."[75] The illustrations from the tour, with the lecture, were published posthumously in 1869.[76] Included among the prints was one of Brigham Young's family. The Mormon seer balanced an infant high over his head in his left hand, held a daughter by the right hand as she stood precariously on his right leg, which rocked another daughter in hobbyhorse fashion (Fig. 18).[77] A fourth child managed somehow to stay perched nonchalantly on his father's left knee. Fourteen other children

72. *Vanity Fair*, 11 February 1860. According to Frank Weitenkampf, H. L. Stephens did the cartoons for *Vanity Fair*. Frank Weitenkampf, *American Graphic Art* (New York: The Macmillan Co., 1942), p. 228.

73. Between 1861 and 1865 there was a grand total of six relatively brief references to the Mormons in *Harper's Weekly*, a far cry from the years 1857–60.

74. *Frank Leslie's Budget of Fun*, September 1865, p. 4. A French periodical did print a vicious engraving by A. Gusmad. See *Le Tour Du Monde* 3 (1862):393.

75. See Richard H. Cracroft, "Distorting Polygamy for Fun and Profit: Artemus Ward and Mark Twain Among the Mormons," *BYU Studies* 14 (Winter 1974):272–88.

76. Even the editors of Ward's published lecture cautioned: "But to most of us Mormonism is still a mystery, and under those circumstances a lecturer who has professedly visited a country for the sake more of picking up fun than of sifting facts, and whose chief object it must be to make his narrative amusing, can scarcely be accepted as an authority." T. W. Robertson and E. P. Hingston, eds., *Artemus Ward's Panorama* (New York: G. W. Carleton, 1869).

77. Ibid., p. 192.

and twelve wives filled in the space of the rest of the picture. Ward's antics helped bring Mormonism back to the attention of the media.[78]

A handful of books illustrated aspects of Mormonism as well. Albert E. Richardson's *Beyond the Mississippi* enlisted several artists to depict western motifs, including some from Utah.[79] Even more influential in continuing to shape the Mormon image was Pomeroy Tucker's 1867 *Origin, Rise and Progress of Mormonism*. In a frontispiece demonstrating that misrepresentation still occurred, the artist changed the gender of the Angel Moroni from male to female, attached wings, pictured a partially nude divine messenger, and created fanciful horned and tailed imps to represent the diabolical (Fig. 19).[80] Although the caption reads "Smith's Account of Taking the Golden Bible from Mormon Hill," none of this resembled Joseph Smith's version of the experience or accurately portrayed his doctrine concerning the nature of angels or devils. These and other books continued to influence the public reputation of Mormonism, although the number of illustrated and written materials substantially lagged behind what was produced in the 1850s.

Fig. 19. "Smith's Account of Taking the Golden Bible from Mormon Hill." Frontispiece to Pomeroy Tucker's *Origin, Rise and Progress of Mormonism* published in 1867.

78. For example, see Betsey Jane Ward, *Hur Book of Goaks* (New York: James O'Kane, 1866). Typical of news dispatches reporting Ward's humor and inspiring pictorial accounts was this brief note: "Artemus Ward writes that he is tired of answering the question as to how many wives Brigham Young has. He says that all he knows about it is that he one day used up the multiplication-table in counting the long-stockings on a clothes-line in Brigham's back yard, and went off feeling dizzy." *Harper's Weekly*, 26 November 1864, p. 755. Also as late as 12 October 1889, Thomas Worth drew his own version of "Brigham Young at Home" from *Artemus Ward's Panorama*. Faithful to his own comic and creative sense, he interpreted the scene somewhat differently. *Texas Siftings*, 12 October 1889.

79. Six different artists represented the Mormons with wood engravings. W. Waud, E. Bonwell, Mary A. Hallock, M. Jarvis, a woman with the last name of Humphrey, and a man by the name of White. Albert D. Richardson, *Beyond the Mississippi* (Hartford, Conn.: American Publishing Company, 1869). See also Samuel Bowles, *Our New West* (Hartford, Conn.: Hartford Publishing Company, 1869). Of course, books published before the Civil War would continue to have an effect on new readers. Travelers' accounts like Richard Burton's *The City of the Saints* (1861) and Jules Remy's *A Journey to Great Salt Lake City* (1861) even defused some negative images.

80. Pomeroy Tucker, *Origin, Rise and Progress of Mormonism* (New York: D. Appleton and Company, 1867), frontispiece. The idea of a female Angel Moroni was perpetuated in Hezekiah Butterworth, *Zig Zag Journeys in the Occident* (Boston: Estes and Lauriant, 1883), p. 258.

2. Sharpening the Visual Image, 1869–1890

After the respite provided during the Civil War and its aftermath, the campaign against polygamy became active again. Both critics and defenders of Mormon marriage practices were equally fervent in their convictions that right was on their side. But the Mormons were hopelessly mismatched, for the press aligned itself foursquare with the opposition to polygamy.

Leslie's Weekly, Harper's Weekly, New Varieties, The Graphic, the early version of *Puck* published in St. Louis, *Frank Leslie's Budget of Fun, Enoch's Advocate*, the New York-based *Puck, Judge, The Wasp, American Punch, Texas Siftings, Chic, Jingo, Sam the Scaramouch*, and *The Daily Graphic*—all these found the Mormons a topic to be treated by their comic artists. Book illustrators, too, were attracted to the subject. The combined output of prints from these and other sources soon eclipsed the volume produced between 1830–69.

The increase in the number of prints produced in the 1870s and 1880s was the result of a number of factors. The completion of the transcontinental railroad, the development of organized anti-Mormon factions, the increasingly sophisticated printmaking technology, and the conflict over polygamy combined to focus national attention on Mormonism.

The railroad brought travelers, but frequently visitors left still ill-informed about Mormonism. Some, however, were favorably impressed. After his stay in Salt Lake City, Frank Leslie, for example, was to vow to represent Mormonism more accurately and objectively.[1] Few came without preconceived notions; many expected a carnival sideshow experience. One French traveler excitedly exclaimed, "Finally we are going to behold those seventeen member households which have only one man."[2] Some observers recognized that their stereotypes required wholesale revision. Others saw what they expected to see.

In addition to greater national exposure after completion of the railroad, pressures on Mormons increased when a pocket of anti-Mormonism blossomed in Utah. Even though this opposition movement was initiated locally, it also played a vital role on the national level. Two factions, disaffected Mormons and hostile non-Mormons, parlayed their antipathy into an anti-

1. Robert Taft, *Artists and Illustrators of the Old West, 1850–1900* (New York: Charles Scribner's Sons, 1953), p. 158.

2. See Wilfried Decoo, "The Image of Mormonism in French Literature: Part I," *BYU Studies* 14 (Winter 1974):172–73.

Mormon political party in 1870.[3] They founded a vigorous medium, the *Salt Lake Tribune*, for the expression of their views.[4] The motivation for this group ran deeper than antagonism over polygamy; economic, political, and ecclesiastical differences fed their resentment.

The national interest in visual portrayals and social commentary that evolved during the Civil War continued. A host of "journals devoted to . . . comic art" now set the stage for the golden age of cartoons, a period spanning the last quarter of the nineteenth century. Technological innovations also made a difference. Cartoonists were no longer limited to working solely in black and white. "A craze for color . . . swept the country."[5] In the pages of *Puck* or *The Wasp* one can trace the chromatic evolution of cartoons on Mormon subjects from black and white through tints to the bold colors of chromolithography. Mormons, like other minorities and causes, found themselves in a cross fire of color and black and white prints from cartoonists operating from coast to coast.

The cartoonists who sketched themselves into notoriety during this postwar generation included Thomas Nast and Joseph Keppler. Joining these two masters of artistic satire were Charles S. Reinhart, Grant Hamilton, C. D. Weldon, A. B. Frost, E. W. Kemble, and Fernando Miranda for *The Daily Graphic*; F. Graetz, Frederick B. Opper, T. Bernard Gillam, Eugene "Zim" Zimmerman, James A. Wales, Dalrymple, Ehrhart, Charles J. Taylor, Joseph Keppler, Jr., L. M. Glackens, Albert Levering, Gordon H. Grant, and Frank Nankivell for *Puck*; Thomas Worth, F. Victor Gillam, and D. McCarthy, among others, for *The Judge*; C. Kendrick for *Chic*; Frederick Keller and Walter for *The Wasp*; and Edward Jump for *Wild Oats*. Some of these and other nationally known artists also decorated books.[6]

From the time it was publicly announced in 1852 until it ceased to exist forty years later, polygamy was the single most popular aspect of Mormonism for artists and writers. When Brigham Young referred to the public announcement of polygamy as "letting the cat out of the bag," he added that "you may expect an eternity of cats . . . for if there is not one thing, there

3. During this early Utah period the territory was not divided according to national party lines. The Liberal Party was the political entity in opposition to the Mormons. The People's Party represented the majority view.

4. For the history of the *Tribune* see O. N. Malmquist, *The First 100 Years: A History of the Salt Lake Tribune, 1871–1971* (Salt Lake City: Utah State Historical Society, 1971).

5. Clarence P. Hornung and Fridolf Johnson, *200 Years of American Graphic Art* (New York: George Braziller, 1976), p. 75.

6. For a competent history of comic artists in the press and a synopsis of book illustration and illustrators see Frank Weitenkampf, *American Graphic Art* (New York: Macmillan, 1924), pp. 179–205, 228–50.

will always be another."[7] Cartoons in this period amply demonstrated the truth of Young's observation.

Phase One—1869–77

The period betwen 1869 and 1890 falls naturally into two phases. The first phase stretches from the joining of the rails in 1869 to the death of Brigham Young in 1877. Several new periodicals marked the introduction of the second phase, which lasted from 1877 until 1890. During the first phase Brigham Young's image remained prominent as the embodiment of Mormonism. Young, or elements surrounding him, frequently became the object of cartoonists and illustrators. Several prints during this 1869–77 phase were produced by traveling artists commissioned by *Harper's Weekly* and *Leslie's Weekly* and artists commissioned to embellish the work of traveling writers like Mark Twain or J. H. Beadle. Three groups from *Leslie's* and *Harper's* sketched their way to the West and back. Finally, former Mormons, such as Fanny Stenhouse, T. B. H. Stenhouse, Ann Eliza Webb Young, and the founders of the anti-Mormon *Salt Lake Tribune* stimulated the production and propagation of numerous prints before 1877.

A few scattered prints of Mormonism appeared in 1869.[8] Many more important illustrations came out the following year when public interest in Mormonism was aroused by the completion of the railroad. Joseph Becker, a staff artist for *Leslie's Weekly*, was one of the first pictorial reporters to make the overland journey by rail.[9] Leaving New York City in mid-October, he spent six weeks in California before taking a side trip from Ogden to Salt Lake as he returned to the East. He sketched "Mormon Converts on Their Way to Salt Lake City," "Members of Brigham Young's Family Buying Fish," "The reserved circle for the wives of Brigham Young in the Mormon theatre," "The Reserved Circle in the Mormon Theatre for the Children of Brigham Young," and other selected scenes (Figs. 20, 21, 22).[10] His drawings appeared in *Leslie's Weekly* on 12 February 1870 in connection with a rather favorable article by Thomas W. Knox. Knox noted the Mormon's industry and temperance, admired their project of building "a magnificent temple," and lauded the Salt Lake Theater.

---

7. *The Journal of Discourses*, 26 vols. (Liverpool, Engl.: Albert Carrington, 1854–86), 1:188.

8. For examples of illustrations in 1869 see T. W. Robertson and E. P. Hingston, eds.) *Artemus Ward's Panorama* (New York: G. W. Carleton, 1869); Samuel Bowles, *Our New West* (Hartford, Conn.: Hartford Publishing Company, 1869); A. K. McClure, *Three Thousand Miles Through the Rocky Mountains* (Philadelphia: J. B. Lippincott & Co., 1869), p. 154; *Nick Nax*, July 1869, p. 69.

9. See Taft, *Artists and Illustrators*.

10. See *Leslie's Weekly*, 29 January, 5 February, and 12 February 1870.

Fig. 20. "Across the Continent.—Mormon Converts on Their Way to Salt Lake City—The Halt on the Road at a Watering Place." *Frank Leslie's Illustrated Newspaper*, 29 January 1870.

Fig. 21. "Across the Continent.—The Fish Market, Salt Lake City—Members of Brigham Young's Family Buying Fish." *Leslie's Weekly*, 5 February 1870.

Fig. 22. "Across the Continent.—Salt Lake City—The Reserved Circle in the Mormon Theatre for the Children of Brigham Young." *Leslie's Weekly*, 12 February 1870.

In contrast to Becker's pictorial report were Charles W. Alexander's *Brigham Young's Daughter* and J. H. Beadle's *Life in Utah*, also published in 1870.[11] The former was faithful to the stock formula and legacy of antebellum anti-Mormon fiction and sensational illustration.[12] The latter, generally borrowing illustrations from other sources, added caustic editorial comments. "If there is any particular development of taste, outside of a few of the cities, any adornment which shows an aspiration for the higher and more beautiful, or any improvements indicating comprehensive grasp and energy of thought," said Beadle, "I have missed them in my travels." He thought Mormonism spoiled the native talents of "the most industrious races of Europe."[13]

In the fall of 1871 Brigham Young was arrested for cohabitation and a trial was scheduled for January 1872. Even before the Civil War, as noted above, the Mormon leader had been a popular target. Now artists were using him as subject matter with increasing regularity. A mischievous color caricature graced the front cover of a songster bearing his name (Fig. 23).[14] *Harper's Weekly* featured him under the heading "The Mormon Troubles—Brigham Young in His Study." Matt Morgan of *Leslie's Weekly* juxtaposed Brigham Young with Ulysses S. Grant in a humorous situation. *New Varieties* showed him in a room packed full of young, comely wives. Now, with a forthcoming trial, nothing could restrain the cartoonists. *Frank Leslie's Budget of Fun* imaginatively walked Brigham Young through the trial from summons to judicial decision.[15] The magazine found him guilty and satirically sentenced him to live with his family for the rest of his life. Actually, before the case came to trial, a higher court ruled that the lower court had exceeded its authority and the Mormon leader went free.

Mormons did not sit idly by during these proceedings. "Twenty-five hundred women of Utah have petitioned the President in favor of polygamy," observed *Harper's Weekly*. "The petitioners urge the removal of the federal officials in Utah, whom they accuse of being 'intent on the destruction of our

Fig. 23. The "Brigham Young Songster." Robert M. De Witt, publisher.

11. C. W. Alexander, *Brigham Young's Daughter* (Philadelphia: C. W. Alexander, 1870); J. H. Beadle, *Life in Utah* (Philadelphia: National Publishing Co., 1870). Beadle was the Utah correspondent for the *Cincinnati Commercial* and editor of the *Salt Lake Reporter*.

12. Novels published earlier during the antebellum period have been studied by Leonard J. Arrington and Jon Haupt, "The Missouri and Illinois Mormons in Ante-Bellum Fiction," *Dialogue: A Journal of Mormon Thought* 5 (Spring 1970):37–50.

13. Beadle, *Life in Utah*, p. 467.

14. *Brigham Young Songster* (New York: Robert M. De Witt Publisher, 1871).

15. *Harper's Weekly*, 25 November 1871, p. 1108; *Leslie's Weekly*, 11 November 1871, p. 137; *New Varieties*, 2 September 1871, p. 9; *Frank Leslie's Budget of Fun*, January 1872, p. 16.

Fig. 24. "The New Departure from Utah. *General Chorus:* 'Good-by, John, Don't Stop Long; Write Back to Your Own Chicabiddies.'" *Frank Leslie's Budget of Fun*, January 1872.

Fig. 25. "Brigham Young the Great American Family Man." *Wild Oats*, 28 March 1872.

honest, happy, industrious and prosperous people' or, at least, the stopping of the 'digraceful court proceedings.' "[16] This popular reaction of the Mormon faithful in support of their leader was the subject of a *Puck* cartoon captioned "The Probable Result of the Mormon Question."[17] A chorus of uniformed Mormon wives, swords in hand, defend their leader as a perplexed Uncle Sam attempts to issue a warrant for his arrest.

The controversy surrounding Brigham Young continued unabated in the media. *Harper's Weekly* reported a rumor that Brigham Young had fled Utah.[18] A cartoon in *Frank Leslie's Budget of Fun* pictured Brigham Young in hasty retreat hotly pursued by irate wives and children (Fig. 24).[19] Meanwhile, *Wild Oats* brutally caricatured him and his wives in a full-page cartoon.[20] Two wives are smoking pipes, one threatens another wife with a knife, one carries a whiskey bottle, and still another is called "the maniac." The sarcasm was not subtle when *Wild Oats* later labeled the Mormon prophet "Brigham Young the Great American Family Man" (Fig. 25).[21]

Just about any pretext was used to lampoon the Mormons and their leader. In 1872 a visit to Salt Lake City by the Japanese ambassador to the United States was such an occasion. Joseph Becker, alias "our Japanese artist, Beckari Nokami," devised the good-natured raillery for *Leslie's Weekly* (Fig. 26).[22] A ten-panel serial cartoon portrayed aggressive Mormon women seeking the ambassador's hand in marriage, the ambassador being formally introduced to Brigham Young's numerous wives, a cocktail party with Mormon elders, a gift to the ambassador of "domestic manufacture"—a Mormon baby, his inspection of a versatile invention which automatically washed and clothed Mormon children, and his "escape" via the Great Salt Lake in a rowboat.

Book illustrations published during the same year were not as humorous. Pictures from William A. Hickman's volume reinforced the textual message that Mormons, especially their leaders, were a violent lot scarcely valuing life.[23] Approaching Mormonism from a different angle was former Mormon Fanny Stenhouse's exposé.[24] The prints in *A Lady's Life Among the Mormons* were by H. L. Stephens, who had been a cartoonist for

16. *Harper's Weekly*, 11 November 1871, p. 1051.

17. *Puck: Illustrierte Wochenschrift*, 1871, p. 12.

18. *Harper's Weekly*, 18 November 1871, p. 1075.

19. *Frank Leslie's Budget of Fun*, January 1872, p. 8.

20. *Wild Oats*, 29 February 1872, p. 4.

21. Ibid., 28 March 1872, p. 16.

22. *Leslie's Weekly*, 24 February 1872, p. 381.

23. William A. Hickman, *Brigham's Destroying Angel* (New York: George A. Crofutt Publisher, 1872).

24. Mrs. T. B. H. Stenhouse, *A Lady's Life Among the Mormons* (New York: American News Company, 1872).

Fig. 26. "The Adventures of the Japanese Ambassador in Utah." *Leslie's Weekly*, 24 February 1872.

the defunct *Vanity Fair*. They showed quarrelsome, unhappy women and impersonal, exploitative Mormon men. The illustrations were based on oversimplification, distortion, and selective attention to blemishes.[25]

Not that humor was entirely abandoned in books.[26] Mark Twain's first edition of *Roughing It* was "fully illustrated by eminent artists."[27] One print showed the inebriating effects of

25. For a scholarly analysis of the effects of polygamy see Stanley S. Ivins, "Notes on Mormon Polygamy," *Western Humanities Review* 10 (Summer 1956):229–39.

26. See John D. Sherwood, *The Comic History of the United States* (Boston: 1870), p. 452. Also later see Livingston Hopkins, *A Comic History of the United States* (New York: American Book Exchange, 1880), p. 197.

27. Mark Twain, *Roughing It* (Hartford, Conn.: American Publishing Co., 1872), p. 126.

Fig. 27. "The Family Bedstead." Illustration from Mark Twain's *Roughing It* published in 1872.

Fig. 28. "I Was Touched." Illustration from Mark Twain's *Roughing It* published in 1872.

"Valley Tan"—"a kind of whiskey, or first cousin to it . . . of Mormon invention . . . made of (imported) fire and brimstone." A second pictured a Mormon "vagrant." "Salt Lake City was healthy," said Twain, "there was only one physician in the place and he was arrested every week regularly and held to answer under the vagrant act for having 'no visible means of support.'" Another portrayed Mormon women, accompanied by an oft-quoted passage:

> I was feverish to plunge in headlong and achieve a great reform here —until I saw the Mormon women. Then I was touched. My heart was wiser than my head. It warmed toward these poor, ungainly, and pathetically "homely" creatures, and as I turned to hide the generous moisture in my eyes, I said, "No—the man that marries one of them has done an act of Christian charity which entitles him to the kindly applause of mankind, not their harsh censure—and the man that marries sixty of them has done a deed of open-handed generosity so sublime that the nations should stand uncovered in his presence and worship in silence."

Nine other illustrations paid their "respects" to Brigham Young, "The Family Bedstead," Mormon children, and other facets of the faith (Figs. 27, 28).

Samuel Clemens had come to mine his own kind of gold in the mountains of Utah. "This was fairyland to us . . . a land of enchantment, and goblins, and awful mystery," wrote the consummate humorist. "We felt a curiosity to ask every child how many mothers it had, and if it could tell them apart; and we experienced a thrill every time a dwelling house door opened and shut as we passed . . . for we longed to have a good satisfying look at a Mormon family in all its comprehensive ampleness. . . ."[28]

28. A careful reading of Twain's *Roughing It* suggests that he questioned some of the "facts" circulating about Mormonism. He spoke of spending a night "in a Gentile den . . . listening to tales"; prefaced one yarn with "according to these Gentile friends of ours," and followed it up with "a Gentile by the name of Johnson . . . gave a preposterous account . . . he embellished rather too much. . . . Some instinct or other made me set this

Then, in 1873, T. B. H. Stenhouse, Fanny Stenhouse's husband, published a copiously illustrated history of Mormonism.[29] While Mormons disagreed with his historical interpretations, like the earlier neutral or objective representations in Charles Mackay's *The Mormons* (published in 1851), the Stenhouse illustrations carried no obvious editorial bias. They were an exception. Prints from other books maintained the more malignant tradition.[30]

In 1873 Ann Eliza Webb Young, one of Brigham Young's wives, sued him for divorce. Cartoonist Thomas Worth quickly envisoned a chain of divorce proceedings.[31] Under the caption "What it is bound to come to," he pictured a United States soldier prodding Brigham Young into divorce court followed by numerous wives (Fig. 29). Failing to receive a settlement for substantial alimony through the judicial system, Ann Eliza Young commenced a crusade against the Mormons, eventually getting aboard the lecture circuit and writing a profusely illustrated book that was a shallow, personal vendetta. The illustrations carried much of her message: Mormonism was a nefarious, stifling system that led its victims into a life of suffering and disillusionment.[32]

Since 1857 no illustrated weekly, with the possible exception of *Leslie's Weekly*, had followed the fortunes of Mormonism more assiduously than *Harper's Weekly*. As interest in Utah, California, and other parts of the West mounted, *Harper's* commissioned two French artists, Paul Frenzeny and Jules Tavernier, to make detailed sketches of a transcontinental expedition beginning in 1873.[33] Their woodcuts can be found sprinkled through-

Fig. 29. "What it is Bound to Come To. *Union Soldier.*—'Come, come, get on into the divorce court. This polygamy business is played out. Here after you chaps can have only one Polly apiece.'" An illustration by Thomas Worth from *Wild Oats*, 13 March 1873.

Johnson down as being unreliable"; finally "we left . . . Salt Lake City . . . not so very much wiser, as regards the Mormon question, than we were when we arrived. . . . We had a deal more 'information' than we had before, of course, but we did not know what portion of it was reliable. . . . All our 'information' had three sides to it, and so I gave up the idea that I could settle the 'Mormon question' in two days. Still I have seen newspaper correspondents do it in one."

29. T. B. H. Stenhouse, *Rocky Mountain Saints* (New York: D. Appleton and Co., 1873). For a more extensive look at the import and nature of these illustrations see Gary L. Bunker and Davis Bitton, "Mormonism Veiled: Establishing the Visual Stereotype, 1830–1850," (unpublished paper in possession of the authors). A large number of these prints dealt with the first few decades of the history of Mormonism.

30. For example, see J. H. Beadle, *The Undeveloped West* (Philadelphia: National Publishing Co., 1873) and Maria Ward, *The Mormon Wife* (Hartford Publishing Co., 1873).

31. *Wild Oats*, 13 March 1873, p. 13. For a more generous caricature of Brigham Young see *The Daily Graphic*, 16 April 1873.

32. Ann Eliza Young, *Wife No. 19* (Hartford, Conn.: Dustin, Gilman & Co., 1876). "Ann Eliza Young, *Wife No. 19, Or the Story of a Life in Bondage*, might have been a revealing report, but this divorced wife of Brother Brigham was too biased to distinguish between fact and fiction." Nels Anderson, *Desert Saints* (Chicago, Ill.: The University of Chicago Press, 1942).

33. Taft, *Artists and Illustrators*, pp. 94–113.

Fig. 30. "Sketches in Utah—Brigham Young's Wives in the Great Mormon Tabernacle." *Harper's Weekly*, 26 September 1874.

Fig. 31. "Enoque's 'Trinity in Unity.' Three Souls with but a Single Thought, Three Heads That Are but One." *Enoch's Advocate*, 18 May 1874.

out the pages of *Harper's* from 1873–75, long after the completion of their assignment. Resembling Joseph Becker's earlier work for their competitor in terms of neutrality of tone, the illustrations were not nearly as callous as the accompanying text. "Mormons at the Communion Table" and "Brigham Young's Wives in the Great Mormon Tabernacle" appeared in 1874 (Fig. 30).[34] "Bringing Home the Fifth Wife" and "A Fresh Supply of Wives Out of the Settlements" and "Reading a Ukase" were published the following year.[35]

When Brigham Young announced the United Order of Enoch in 1874, the local anti-Mormon movement in Salt Lake City reacted to the United Order's principles by producing an illustrated periodical satirically entitled *Enoch's Advocate*.[36] Brigham Young's economic innovations were based on the ideal of self-sufficiency, and he desired his people's total independence from imported goods or the services of others. Even locally-produced wooden shoes, he thought, ought to be considered. Although no effort was ever made to insist that Mormons wear wooden shoes, they were promoted in places like Hebron, Utah.[37] Opponents of the United Order seized upon the idea of wooden shoes as a means of ridiculing the whole self-sufficiency program, and they became the central symbol of mockery for *Enoch's Advocate*. Of the twelve illustrations appearing in the six issues, seven carried out the wooden-shoe theme. Six featured Brigham Young. As a group the prints were as biting as any set of illustrations produced to that date. Brigham Young was shown milking an animal emblematic of the so-called "superstitious" Mormon people; as an octopus; imposing wooden shoes on the editor of the *Salt Lake Herald*; and barred from entry to heaven as a result of questionable financial entanglements (Figs. 31, 32, 33, 34). *Enoch's Advocate* went to extreme lengths to malign Brigham Young. It cartooned his death as "A Solution

34. *Harper's Weekly*, 26 September 1874, p. 793.

35. Ibid., 2 January 1875, p. 4; 30 January 1875, p. 97; 6 February 1875, p. 109.

36. One of the earliest illustrated periodicals in the Great Basin was the *Keep-A-Pitchinin*, a humorous, satirical publication supporting the claims of Mormonism. Nine lines mention this periodical in J. Cecil Alter, *Early Utah Journalism* (Salt Lake City: Utah State Historical Society, 1938), p. 272. Also see Ronald W. Walker, "The Keep-A-Pitchinin or the Mormon Pioneer was Human," *BYU Studies* 14 (Spring 1974):331–44. In part the appearance of *Enoch's Advocate* may have been a reaction to the feisty model of the *Keep-A-Pitchinin*. For more extensive study of the visual image projected by *Enoch's Advocate* see Davis Bitton and Gary L. Bunker, "*Enoch's Advocate* (1874): A Forgotten Satirical Periodical," (unpublished paper in possession of the authors).

37. In Hebron, Utah, Orson W. Huntsman found the wood "Order shoes" uncomfortable and traded some potatoes to an Indian for a pair of moccasins. The moccasins, said Huntsman, "took the shine off the old wooden shoes for comfort and handsomeness." Anderson, *Desert Saints*, p. 388.

to Many Problems." One caricature showed the First Presidency of the church symbolically clad in one body and a single pair of wooden shoes, the hand of the Trustee-in-Trust in his pocket.

In 1875 local anti-Mormon sympathies were expressed again through cartoons in the *Salt Lake Tribune* when Samuel B. Axtell, the new federally-appointed governor of Utah, tried to steer a neutral course midway between the Mormon-baiters and the Mormons.[38] Since neutrality was anathema to the anti-Mormon "Gentile Ring," Axtell soon found himself subjected to a relentless attack by non-Mormons. They sarcastically dubbed him "bishop" and caricatured him as a turncoat ally of Mormonism. In *Tribune* cartoons Axtell appeared as the puppet of Brigham Young "lubricated with Axtell grease . . . to run my way." He was even maliciously implicated as a participant in polygamy.[39]

Nationally, passage of the Poland Act (which modified the territorial judicial system and increased federal control), the conviction of the polygamist George Reynolds, and the arrest and trial of church member John D. Lee for his part in the Mountain Meadows Massacre kept Mormonism before the public. In 1876, while book illustrations flourished, periodical print exposure tapered off considerably.[40] Then two events stimulated a resurgence of graphic preoccupation with Mormonism in the illustrated weeklies in 1877. The first was the excursion to the West of Frank and Miriam Leslie and their party. The second was the death of Brigham Young.

The Leslie group left New York in April . The party of twelve included *Leslie* writers, a photographer, and two staff artists, Harry Ogden and Walter R. Yeager,[41] all committed to recording both visual and verbal impressions. Frank Leslie was the publisher of more than a dozen periodicals, one of which sold

Fig. 32. "Effects of Stripping the Last Teat." *Enoch's Advocate,* 7 May 1874.

Fig. 33. "The Cephalopod of the Great Basin.—*Genus Polypi Mormoni Priesthoodi.*" *Enoch's Advocate,* 11 May 1874.

Fig. 34. "The Ascension of Enoch the Second. And Enoch the Second Was Not for the Heavens Took Him. Tune: Hail to the Prophet Ascending to Heaven." *Enoch's Advocate,* 6 June 1874.

38. *Salt Lake Tribune,* 28 February 1875; 7 March 1875; 21 March 1875. As vitriolic as these cartoons were, they did not exhibit the poor taste shown by the *Tribune* in the case involving the City Marshal. A resolution from the City Council had excluded a *Tribune* reporter from future Council deliberations. Incensed, the newspaper gave front-page billing to the episode. The City Marshal, who had delivered the decisions of exclusion, became the butt of jesting. Over the caption "The City Marshal" appeared a portrait of a man also regularly included in a patent medicine advertisement in the same newspaper promising to cure gonorrhea, syphilis, and other venereal disease. See *Salt Lake Tribune,* 15 September 1875, for the *Tribune* reaction and compare with the patent medicine advertisement (which also probably appeared earlier) on 7 October 1875.

39. After five months in office, Samuel B. Axtell accepted a federal judgeship in New Mexico.

40. Ann Eliza Young's book was the most noteworthy illustrated publication of 1876. Travelers also continued their illustrated reports. See R. and G. D. Hook, *Through Dust and Foam: Or Travels Sight-seeing, and Adventure by Land and Sea in the Far West and Far East* (Hartford, Conn.: Columbia Book Co., 1876). We have only one print from illustrated weeklies in our collection for 1876.

41. See Taft, *Artists and Illustrators.*

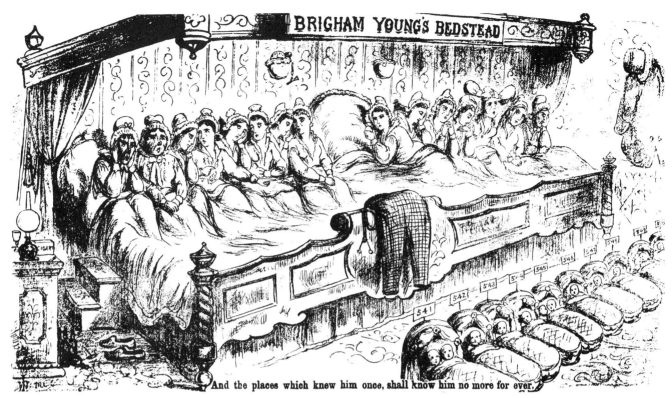

Fig. 35. "This Shop to Let." Printed and sold by
E. Smith & Co.

Fig. 36. "Brigham Young's Successors:—New Rule. Last Into Bed
Put Out the Light." Printed by J. Marks.

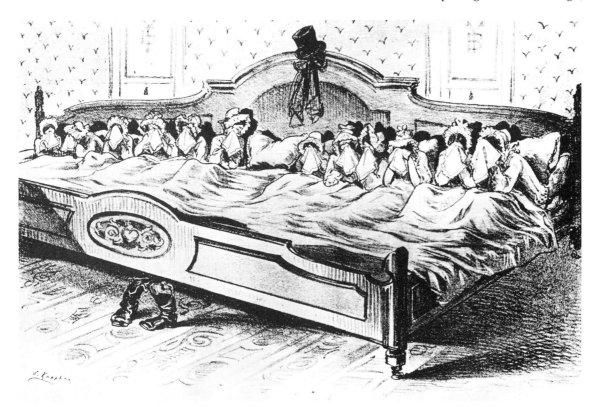

Fig. 37. "In Memorium Brigham Young. 'And the Place Which Knew Him Once Shall Know Him No More.'" *Puck*, 5 September 1877.

as many as four hundred thousand copies per issue. His gifted, articulate wife took a hand in the publishing business and wrote a detailed exposition of the journey. On the way back, they took the opportunity to personally interview Brigham Young. Whether from the interview or other observations during their visit to the citadel of Mormonism, the Leslies came away favorably impressed. "I for one do not want to see them treated with injustice," said Frank Leslie.[42]

Later that year, 29 August 1877, Brigham Young died. While the Mormons mourned the loss of their leader, the press generally welcomed the event.[43] *Puck* marked the occasion with four cartoons over a six-week period. Separately published comic prints, from as far away as the British Isles, were sold at home and abroad (Figs. 35, 36, 37).[44] In an exception to this pattern, *Leslie's Weekly* published a temperate piece tastefully illustrated by two prints.[45]

---

42. Ibid., p. 158; Mrs. Frank Leslie, *California: A Pleasure Trip from Gotham to the Golden Gate* (New York, 1877; reprint, 1972).

43. See Gary L. Bunker and Davis Bitton, "The Death of Brigham Young: Occasion for Journalistic Revel," in preparation.

44. These prints can be found in the graphic arts collection at Yale University.

45. *Leslie's Weekly*, 23 November 1878, pp. 196–97, 207; *Puck*, 15

Fig. 38. "A Distinction without a Difference. *Justice.* 'As the laws now stand, Mr. Jonathan, we can punish a Gentile bigamist, but in the case of a Mormon polygamist they appear to be inoperative. Is that right?' *Mormon.* 'I am not a criminal. Polygamy is a part of my Church creed. No interference of State with Church, you know. I—' *Jonathan.* 'Stop, sir! Your plea is but a sham, to cover a heinous crime that should be tolerated no longer. If the laws are inadequate, they must be seen to. Nearly twenty years ago I wiped out slavery; now it is about time to attend to you.'" *Harper's Weekly*, 30 April 1881, drawn by Gillam.

Phase Two—1877–90

The second phase of graphic development, 1877–90, was sparked by new periodicals beginning with and modeled after *Puck. The Judge* and *The Wasp* were the most notable additions. Fewer prints came from short-lived periodicals like *American Punch, Chic, Jingo, Sam the Scaramouch,* and *Texas Siftings.* Add the graphics from the durable weeklies *Harper's* and *Leslie's* and those appearing in *The Daily Graphic,* and a formidable number of illustrations resulted. Book illustrations continued to appear. Four more exposés, a dime novel, a "scientific" exposition, and other works appeared in 1882 alone, a high-water mark for anti-Mormon illustration.

Now that Brigham Young was gone, church president John Taylor attracted most of the pictorial attention, although cartoonists occasionally brought back Young's image. Between 1877–90, pictorial portrayals of Mormonism were qualitatively more negative and more frequent.

Pictorially, 1878 passed inconspicuously. Except for some scenes of Mormons arriving at Castle Garden, the Ellis Island of the nineteenth century, and John Taylor's debut in *Puck,* illustrators ignored Mormonism.[46]

In 1879, Secretary of State William M. Evarts sought sanction from foreign governments against Mormon evangelism abroad and the immigration of Mormon converts. *The Daily Graphic* on 15 October 1879 put the following doggerel in Evarts' mouth:

> I want you to see
> That every—e—e
> Man who migrates
> To the United States
> Has no more than one wife
> To trouble his life
> For it is not a good plan
> For a single man
> To Marry and carry
> A harem with him.
> I've promised some ladies
> O'er a cup of Bohea
> To stop import of Mormons
> From over the sea.

None of this amused the Mormons. Still fresh on their minds was the death of one of their missionaries, Joseph Standing, who

May 1878, pp. 8–9; Mormonism was also depicted in the background of an illustration captioned "Arion Masquerade Ball" in *Puck,* 20 February 1878. A few other illustrations, copies of previously published prints, appeared in: John Henry Barrows, "Christian Education for the Mormons: from prelude to the 118th Lecture in Monday Lectureship," *Boston Advertiser Report,* 25 December 1878, and William Preston Johnston, *The Life of General Albert Sidney Johnston* (New York: D. Appleton & Co., 1878).

46. *Leslie's Weekly,* 23 November 1878; *Puck,* 15 May 1878.

Fig. 39. "Situations of the Mormons in Utah." Drawn by Keller for
The Wasp, 1 February 1879.

Fig. 40. "Utah Defiant—The Mormon Commander Mustering His
Forces," which included, clockwise from the upper left, "The Old
Guard," "The Infant-ry," and the "Knife-and-Fork Brigade." *Puck*,
14 January 1880, drawn by J. Keppler.

Fig. 41. "The Opposition Tabernacles. *Brother Taylor to Brother Talmage*: People Who Live in Brooklyn Houses Shouldn't Throw Stones!" *Puck*, 6 October 1880, drawn by J. Keppler.

Fig. 42. "Violators of the Laws of the Land. Columbia: 'Even (G. Q.) Cannon shall not open these doors to you.'" *Harper's Weekly*, 28 February 1882, by Thomas Nast.

Fig. 43. "The Carrion Crow in the Eagle's Nest." Drawn by Victor Gillam for *Puck*, 25 January 1882.

Fig. 44. "A Desperate Attempt to Solve the Mormon Question," *Puck*, 13 February 1884. Clockwise from the upper left, "I think one wife is enough," by Gillam, "How long will this destructive monster be allowed to live?" by Opper, "What is the use of Mormonism when a man can change his wife whenever he wants?" by Graetz, and "I imagine it must be perfect Paradise," by Keppler.

had been shot by a mob just three months earlier. In early 1879 the Supreme Court, upholding the conviction of polygamist George Reynolds, denied that freedom of religion could be claimed by those involved in this practice that was contrary to the mores of American society. In another case that same court reversed the conviction of Owen Miles for practicing polygamy. The only evidence of a marriage between Miles and Emily Spencer had been the testimony of Carrie Owen Miles, which was inadmissible since a husband or wife could not testify against each other. Irritation at the Miles ruling was pictorially expressed by Bernard Gillam, a cartoonist for *Harper's Weekly* (Fig. 38).[47] Subtle nuances in the facial features, hands, and

47. *Harper's Weekly*, 30 April 1881, p. 289. Bernard Gillam "found his true calling" as a political cartoonist. "In 1800 he worked with Nast on *Harper's Weekly* and the following year left to join the staff of *Puck*. In 1886 he became part owner of the reorganized *Judge*, for whom he did some of his famous and influential cartoons." Ron Tyler, *The Image of America in Caricature & Cartoon* (Fort Worth, Texas: Amon Carter Museum of Western Art, 1976).

Fig. 45. "Uncle Sam in Mormondom. 'If those fellows will half-mast my colors it behooves me to rise upon my dignity with a club.'" Cover from *Sam the Scaramouch*, 18 July 1885, by Porter.

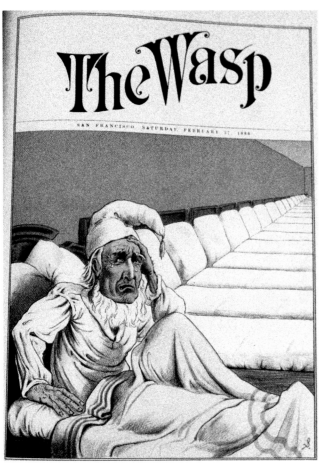

Fig. 46. "The Mormon Begins to Feel Lonesome."
The Wasp, 27 February 1886.

Fig. 47. "Mormon View of the New Fortress." *The
Wasp*, 14 August 1886, by Walter.

Fig. 48. "Gentiles of Salt Lake City Capture the
Mormon Stronghold." *The Wasp*, 22 February 1890.

profile appealed to the reader's emotions, the captioned dialogue did the rest:

Justice: As the laws now stand, Mr. Jonathan, we can punish a Gentile bigamist, but in the case of a Mormon polygamist they appear to be inoperative. Is that right?

Mormon: I am not a criminal. Polygamy is a part of my Church creed. No interference of State with Church, you know. I—

Jonathan: Stop, sir! Your plea is but a sham, to cover a heinous crime that should be tolerated no longer. If the laws are inadequate, they must be seen to. Nearly twenty years ago I wiped out slavery; now it is about time to attend to you.

Leslie's Weekly picked up on another aspect of the Miles litigation. Mormon leader Daniel Wells had refused, as a matter of conscience, to answer certain questions at the lower court hearing. A contempt of court citation brought a fine and a brief stay in jail. However, when he was released he came home to a hero's welcome, including a full-fledged parade and celebration before a packed house in the Tabernacle. *Leslie's* recorded that event in multiple sketches.[48]

A cartoon by *The Wasp's* Frederick Keller summarized the explosive situation in 1879 (Fig. 39).[49] Uncle Sam observed a keg of "Congress Powder" ready for detonation under John Taylor's "polygamy house." Only time delayed the ignition of the fuse.

Barely into a new decade, *Puck* featured a roosterized John Taylor in a colorful fold-out lithograph surrounded by militant Mormon women (Fig. 40).[50] Keppler returned to the Mormon president later that year when De Witt Talmage leveled a blast at the Mormons (Fig. 41).[51] Only Keppler's greater dislike for Talmage tempered the image of Taylor with his wives. Out in San Francisco *The Wasp* used a trite motif by showing polygamy as a painful tooth being extracted. In the background hung the extracted tooth of slavery, evoking the caption: "Force of Example—Pull—Gamey and It Must Come."[52] In 1881 two inaugural addresses—the second occasioned by the assassination of President Garfield—demanded firm action against polygamy and instigated a flurry of assenting cartoons from *Chic, Leslie's Weekly, Harper's Weekly, The Judge, Puck,* and *The Daily Graphic.*

There were a few exceptions to the outpouring against the Mormons. *The Wasp* urged moderation and tolerance. It commended a George Q. Cannon article to fair-minded readers,

48. *Leslie's Weekly*, 31 May 1879, pp. 214–15.
49. *The Wasp*, 1 February 1879, pp. 424–25.
50. *Puck*, 14 January 1880, pp. 526–27.
51 *Puck*, 6 October 1880, p. 82.
52. *The Wasp*, 10 January 1880, p. 82.

urged greater self-awareness to "Mormon-haters"; chastized "the brawling bawds of the *Salt Lake Tribune*"; decried the falsehood, stupidity, and injustice" perpetrated by "the brutal . . . mob of scribblers . . . who find profit in denouncing"; and paralleled the religious persecution of the Mormons with like accusations "against the Jews in Castile, the Parsees in Persia, the Waldenees in Piedmont, the Puritans in England and the Quakers in Massachusetts." "Excepting the Jews and the Chinese," *The Wasp* found "no worthier large class of people than the Mormons"—which, considering the prejudice directed against Jews and Orientals, was not exactly complimentary.[53]

In 1882, when Utah Governor Eli H. Murray ignored the landslide results of the election of George Q. Cannon as a delegate from Utah Territory and certified his opponent as the winner, the issue was sent to the House of Representatives. Prints graphically chronicled Cannon's exclusion. *Leslie's* called it the "recoil of the Cannon."[54] Also using the cannon as an obvious symbol, Thomas Nast did a before-after sequence for *Harper's* (Fig. 42).[55]

Early 1882 also brought an avalanche of illustrations anticipating or celebrating the signing of the anti-polygamy Edmunds Act by President Chester A. Arthur.[56] Mormons were shown abusing their own immigrants.[57] Withdrawing voting privileges from those believing in or practicing polygamy, one of the act's provisions, was applauded.[58] One cartoon pictured Utah as the black carrion crow in a nest of otherwise white eaglets representing the states of the United States under the protection of the American eagle (Fig. 43).[59]

If the Mormons' image in periodicals was bad in 1882, the graphic impression in books was worse. *Sweet William, The*

---

53. *The Wasp*, 30 April 1881, p. 276. For content of similar tone see 14 August 1880, p. 21; 26 March 1881, p. 196; 2 April 1881, p. 210. "A Gentile newspaper correspondent at Salt Lake City has the happiness to be sourly disaffected toward Mormonism. He says: 'It is a blot upon the face of the earth, particularly in this lovely valley, so green and beautiful with apple, peach, pear, and palm trees in full blossom—grass swaying in the wind, bees humming, and birds singing, like our July weather; while just beyond all this in the background are the mountains covered with snow. In this charming picture the only objects not directly created by Mormonism are the mountains covered with snow." Ibid., 25 June 1881, p. 405.

54. *Leslie's Weekly*, 29 April 1882, p. 160.

55. *Harper's Weekly*, 28 February 1882, p. 61; 6 May 1882, p. 288.

56. *Leslie's Weekly, Harper's Weekly, The Judge, Puck, The Wasp,* and *The Daily Grapic* all chipped in multiple cartoons.

57. See *Leslie's Weekly*, 11 February 1882, pp. 432–33; and 11 March 1882, cover.

58. *The Judge*, 4 March 1882, pp. 8–9.

59. *Puck*, 25 January 1882, p. 340; "This 'peculiar people' is as much out of place among our people as a carrion-crow is out of place in an eagle's nest," exclaimed the editorial comment. Ibid., p. 326.

Trapper Detective, one of Erasmus Beadle's dime novels, featured a hooded Mormon vigilante committee on its cover.[60] The dime novel, though espousing morality themes, had degenerated into "sensationalism, violence, and over-wrought emotionalism."[61] Paralleling the dime novel was a series of publications sponsored by the *National Police Gazette*, a periodical hardly noted for staid decorum. A volume in the series, a profusely illustrated *Mysteries of Mormonism*, reveled in the bizarre, extravagant distortion, and pure fabrication.[62] Other unflattering book illustrations sated the appetite of curiosity seekers.[63] Meanwhile, *Physiognomy Illustrated* provided a scientific explanation: the narrow aperture of the Mormon eye caused a penchant for polygamy.[64]

During the latter half of 1882 and even the first three quarters of 1883, periodical artists abandoned the "Mormon problem" for other issues, apparently feeling that the fate of Mormonism was sealed. When the new law failed to produce the desired change, however, the media resumed its pictorial barrage. From October 15, 1883, through December, *The Daily Graphic* deplored the Mormon situation with almost weekly full-page cover spreads. A cartoon in *Texas Siftings* threatened to turn loose a fighting cock dressed as an American soldier against the banty Mormon rooster.[65] *The Wasp* pictured a perplexed Uncle Sam reading proposals from a pile of manuscripts offering variant solutions to the problem.[66] As he read, an endless line of mail carriers dumped more suggestions in his lap. Outside the window a few Mormon males could be seen shepherding a long line of women behind the walls of Salt Lake City. The Mormons did not have ready access to the media; no pro-Mormon cartoons counteracted the anti-Mormon images.

60. Joseph E. Badger, Jr., *Sweet William, The Trapper Detective* (New York: Beadle & Adams, Publishers, 1882).

61. Russel Nye, *The Unembarrassed Muse* (New York: The Dial Press, 1970), p. 61.

62. Alfred Trumble, *The Mysteries of Mormonism* (New York: Police Gazette, 1882). This was just one of a series of sensational booklets published by the *National Police Gazette*. Others appeared under such cities as: *Glimpses of Gotham, New York by Day and Night, Paris by Gaslight, The Mysteries of New York, Secrets of the Stage and Folly's Queens.*

63. For example, see J. W. Buel, *Metropolitan Life Unveiled: Or the Mysteries and Miseries* (St. Louis, Chicago, Atlanta: Anchor Publishing Co., 1882) and John D. Lee, *Mormonism Unveiled* (Lewisburg, Pa.: S. T. Buck Son & Co., 1882). The latter included several prints in color.

64. Joseph Simms, *Physiognomy Illustrated or Nature's Revelations of Character* (New York: Murray Hill, 1882), pp. 158–64. For a more extensive treatment of similar explanations see Gary L. Bunker and Davis Bitton, "Polygamous Eyes: A Note on Mormon Physiognomy," *Dialogue: A Journal of Mormon Thought* 12 (Autumn 1979):114–19.

65. *Texas Siftings*, 8 December 1883, p. 16.

66. *The Wasp*, 1 December 1883, p. 16.

In 1884, although the flood of book illustrations showed no signs of drying up,[67] cartoons from periodicals were down by more than half from the previous year. *Jingo* and *The Judge* caricatured the Mormons, but as a means to another end— a political attack on Grover Cleveland.[68] *Puck*, somehow reluctant to abandon a topic so natural to the production of humor, published four Mormon cartoons combined as a unit on a double-page lithograph (Fig. 44).[69] Four artists—Joseph Keppler, Bernard Gillam, Frederick Opper and F. Graetz—drew themselves as central or peripheral figures in their own versions of the Mormon setting. A humorous verse accompanied the coordinated print:

> Four artists who differ in style and in mind,
> This cartoon on the Mormons have jointly designed.
> The results of their labor is here—and what's more,
> We'll remark that in Utah they laugh at all four.

In 1885 caricatured Mormons appeared in *The Daily Graphic*, *Harper's Weekly*, *The Judge*, *Puck*, *The Wasp*, and, a new entry, *Sam the Scaramouch*. Many of the cartoons were provoked by a minor but provocative incident. Protesting what they considered the abrogation of their civil and religious liberties, the Mormons had half-masted the American flag on the Fourth of July. A cartoon on the cover of *Sam the Scaramouch* on 18 July showed half-masted flags on the spires of the temple, the tabernacle, and a prominent flag pole between the two edifices (Fig. 45). "If those fellows will half-mast my colors," noted Uncle Sam in the caption, "it behooves me to rise upon my dignity with a club." Incredibly, a later issue compared the incident to the firing on Fort Sumter at the commencement of the Civil War. "Put the Mormons out," exclaimed Sam.[70] *Texas Siftings* was equally indignant.[71]

---

67. See Marietta Holly, *My Wayward Pardner: Or, My Trials With Josiah, America, The Widow Bump, and Etcetery* (Hartford, Conn.: American Publishing Company, 1884); William L. Spencer, *Salt Lake Fruit* (Boston: Franklin Press, 1884); and William Jarman, *Uncle Sam's Abscess; Or, Hell Upon Earth* (Exeter, Engl.: 1884).

68. See *Jingo* 17 September 1884, p. 20, and 22 October 1884, p. 112; and *The Judge*, 25 October 1884, p. 3, and 1 November 1884, pp. 8–9.

69. *Puck*, 13 February 1884, pp. 376–77. These are the only four cartoons from *Puck* that we know of for this year.

70. "The Mormon Elders have not as yet been called to account for halfmasting the American flag on the Fourth of July. There is as much provocation in this as there was on firing on Fort Sumter. The Mormon Elders should be moved out of the country, house, foot, dragoons, wives, twins and triplets. The effluvia of polygamy is rising from Salt Lake City. Talk about London and the Pall Mall Gazette! We trust the next Democratic Governor of Utah may be a South Carolina fire-eater of monogamic tendencies, and as much backbone as President Cleveland. Put the Mormons out!" *Sam the Scaramouch*, 1 August 1885, p. 358. There was more of the same in the next week's issue of 8 August 1885, p. 374.

71. Over the half-masting affair *Texas Siftings* remonstrated: "The Gentiles have been exasperated to a point where they may be led into violence at almost any time." *Texas Siftings*, 22 August 1885, p. 2.

Locally the mood was as menacing. On 10 July 1885 the *Salt Lake Tribune* threatened an ugly confrontation if the Mormons repeated the incident in their own forthcoming territorial celebration of Pioneer Day on 24 July. A patriotic crowd from the mining camps "would probably result in a speedy effectual settlement of the whole Mormon business." The Mormons threw down their own gauntlet saying that the flags would be half-masted. A curious coincidence defused the tension. Out of respect for the death of former President Ulysses S. Grant, an executive order for half-masting all American flags, beginning 23 July, was issued from the White House.[72]

In 1886 a poster offered $500 for information leading to the arrest of George Q. Cannon, a "fugitive from justice" who, according to *Leslie's Weekly*, "has long figured as the brains of the Mormon Church."[73] Like many other Mormon polygamists, Cannon had gone "underground." Soon the relentless pursuit paid dividends. While traveling incognito on a train in Nevada, he was identified and arrested. *The Judge* gave a colorful description of his capture. "George Q. Cannon jumped from a moving train to get away from the sheriff who had him in charge, and broke his nose. A man who has lived a long period with eight or ten wives is necessarily a brave man; but if he doesn't know better than to jump so as to strike on his nose he had far better be a coward."[74] *The Wasp* featured Cannon in a front-page color cartoon (Fig. 46).[75] Numerous empty beds next to him explained why "The Mormon Begins to Feel Lonesome." This sense of satisfaction over Cannon's arrest soon turned sour when Cannon jumped bail to return to life on the underground.

The Edmunds-Tucker bill of 1887 abolished female suffrage, deprived the wives of polygamists of immunity from testifying against their husbands, dissolved the church as a corporation, eliminated the Perpetual Emigrating Fund, which had financed emigrants to the Salt Lake Valley, and instructed the Utah Supreme Court to escheat all church property with the exception of houses of worship. *The Wasp* expressed its confidence that the political pressures were taking their calculated toll in a cartoon that envisioned the gentiles taking control of the "Mormon Fortress"—Salt Lake City (Fig. 47).[76]

From 1888 to 1890 few illustrations of Mormons appeared in the media.[77] In 1890, a final cartoon on Mormonism was

---

72. See Anderson, *Desert Saints*, p. 326.

73. Cannon's visibility as Territorial Representative to the Congress from Utah and his role as defender of the faith in the media probably earned him this reputation. See *Leslie's Weekly*, 29 April 1882, p. 160.

74. *The Judge*, 6 March 1886, p. 12.

75. *The Wasp*, 27 February 1886, p. 1.

76. Ibid., 14 August 1886, p. 16.

77. Only about thirteen cartoons appeared in illustrated weeklies from 1887 to 1890. Arthur Conan Doyle's first edition of *A Study in Scarlet*, appearing in 1887, was illustrated by George Hutchinson and James Greig.

published in *The Wasp* (Fig. 48).[78] When Mormons lost their right to exercise their political franchise, the anti-Mormon Liberal Party seized political control of Salt Lake City. "Gentiles of Salt Lake City Capture the Mormon Stronghold," stated the cartoon caption. In the fall of that year, Mormon church President Wilford Woodruff issued the Manifesto announcing the cessation of polygamy.

"Nothwithstanding the frequency with which the American Press has kept the name of the Mormons before the public," wrote T. B. H. Stenhouse in 1873, "few persons have any definite idea of what Mormonism claims to be, and what it actually is."[79] His statement was just as valid in 1890. After years of press coverage the public knew almost nothing of what Mormonism claimed to be or what it actually was. But the media had produced a powerful image of Mormonism. Like all such stereotypes it was a caricature. Selective, one-sided, unfair, the image was nevertheless what most people believed about the Mormons. Such are the ingredients of prejudice.

See the facsimile copy of the original edition Arthur Conan Doyle, *A Study in Scarlet* (New York: Hart Publishing Company, 1976). The line drawings in this version were rendered after the originals by Joseph A. Brown.

78. *The Wasp*, 22 February 1890, pp. 10–11.

79. T. B. H. Stenhouse, *Rocky Mountain Saints*, p. iii.

Harper's Weekly and *Leslie's Weekly* dominated the illustrated periodical market until 1869. The comic weeklies like *Puck*, *The Judge*, and *The Wasp* flourished in the second phase, 1869–90. Between 1890 and 1914 newspaper cartoon predominated.[1] Most of the important dailies hired their own cartoonists or borrowed cartoons from other newspapers or did both.

The pressures of a daily deadline led artists to produce pen-and-ink drawings rather than the more laborious and detailed prints produced by the magazines. These simplified line drawings made it possible to increase the number of cartoons and augmented the capacity of newspapers to shape the image of Mormonism.

Newspaper cartoonists quickly established their reputations alongside those of their artistic peers who drew for the weeklies. Charles Nelan (*New York Herald*), C. G. Bush (*New York World*), Homer Davenport (*New York Journal*), Clifford Berryman (*Washington Post*), C. L. "Bart" Bartholomew (*Minneapolis Journal*), and R. C. Bowman (*Minneapolis Tribune*) included Mormonism among the many subjects of their distinctive pictorial editorials.[2]

In terms of sheer numbers no other newspaper could equal the *Salt Lake Tribune* when it came to cartoons about Mormonism. Some eight hundred cartoons focused on the Mormons during this period with more than six hundred of these appearing in the four years from 1905 to 1909.

Newspapers published the majority of illustrations on Mormons during this period. Magazine cartoons appeared less frequently. *The Judge*, *The Wasp*, *Harper's Weeekly*, and *Leslie's Weekly* generally ignored the Mormons. But other weeklies, mainly *Puck* and *Life*, continued the comic tradition.[3] These two periodicals humored their patrons with generalized images and were less tied to the news events that generated cartoons in newspapers. In addition, a few illustrated anti-Mormon pamph-

3. Uneasy Accommodation, 1890–1914

1. See Allen Nevins and Frank Weitenkampf, *A Century of Political Cartoons* (New York: Charles Scribner's Sons, 1944), pp. 11, 15–16; William Murrell, *A History of American Graphic Humor*, 2 vols. (New York: Cooper Square Publishers, Inc., 1967); Stephen Becker, *Comic Art in America* (New York: Simon Schuster, 1959); Stephen Hess and Milton Kaplan, *The Ungentlemanly Art: A History of American Political Cartoons* (New York: Macmillan Co., 1968).

2. Frank Weitenkampf, *American Graphic Art* (New York: Macmillan Co., 1924).

3. Cartoons in *Puck* on the Mormons appeared between 1904–7. *Life* published a few between 1904–6.

lets, monthly and quarterly periodicals, and illustrated books added to the cumulative image of Mormonism.

Tempering the National Image, 1890–97

With the church authorizing no new polygamous marriages, at least officially, tensions were reduced and attitudes toward the Mormons improved as reciprocal concessions were tendered. For the Mormons, political realignment along traditional national party lines symbolized this conciliatory spirit. Revamping judicial procedures, secularizing public education, and altering some economic policies were outward manifestations of the desire for statehood.[4] President Benjamin Harrison granted amnesty to those currently under penalty for violation of polygamy statutes; Harrison's successor, Grover Cleveland, restored the voting franchise. Statehood was granted in 1896.

Until 1898 the Mormons seemed to be melting into the national landscape more easily and were less interesting as cartoon subjects. There are only a few examples from this era as the number of prints dwindled.[5]

This change in attitude is evidenced by an 1897 installment in the popular Frank Merriwell series by Gilbert Patten.[6] On the surface "Frank Merriwell Among the Mormons or The Lost Tribe of Israel" appeared to be a restatement of familiar motifs. The color print on the front page of *Tip Top Weekly* did not suggest any change in attitudes (Fig. 49). Elder Asaph Holdfast, the Mormon villain, was shown rejecting Merriwell's modern mode of transportation, the bicycle, as he exclaimed: "Remove from my sight those inventions of Satan!" The name "Holdfast" and the "thees" and "thous" sprinkled liberally in his pattern of spech buttressed the anti-progressive image. The

4. See Gustive O. Larson, *The "Americanization" of Utah for Statehood* (San Marino, Calif.: The Huntington Library, 1971).

5. See Gen. John Eaton, LL.D., "The Mormons of To-day," a series of articles from the *Christian Herald*, pamphlet issued 23 August 1897. From microfilm at Brigham Young University of the Berrian Collection at the New York Public Library. The frontispiece showed an octopus straddling the State of Utah and extending its tentacles to other states. Between 1890 and 1897 our search has only turned up a few cartoons from *Life, The Judge, Tip Top Weekly,* and the *Salt Lake Tribune.* Scattered illustrations also occasionally appeared in other periodicals and books. For example, Kate Tannatt Woods, *Across the Continent* (Boston: Lathrop Publishing Company [ca. 1897]), p. 189. From illustrated periodicals see Alvah Milton Kerr, "American Dead Sea Fruit," *Overland Monthly,* "Fatal Blunder," *Overland Monthly* (August 1896), pp. 182–87.

6. "Frank Merriwell Among the Mormons or the Lost Tribe of Israel," *Tip Top Weekly* 1 (June 19, 1897). Creator Gilbert Patten generally wrote under the nom de plume Brut L. Standish. Within three months after its introduction in 1896 the *Tip Top Weekly* attained a circulation of 75,000. See Bill Blackbeard, "That Nonpareil All-American Boy Reaches 80," *Smithsonian* 7 (June 1976):80–85. On the Frank Merriwell series see also Russel Nye, *The Unembarrassed Muse* (New York: The Dial Press, 1974), pp. 74–75.

Fig. 49. "Frank Merriwell Among the Mormons."
Tip Top Weekly, 19 June 1897.

text explained that old Holdfast was more than dated. His "evil nature," revealed "in his narrow little eyes," set him at odds against Merriwell, the embodiment of American values. The plot, a stock formula, pictured Holdfast jeopardizing the freedom of a young Mormon maiden to select the mate of her choice. Holdfast wanted her for himself. Melodramatically, the all-American Frank Merriwell and associates snatch her from Holdfast's grasp just in the nick of time.

But there is a new element in the story, for the young lady's suitor, Tom Whitcomb, represents a new type of Mormon. His modern name contrasts with Asaph Holdfast's, as does his deportment and religious world view. With the able and moral Tom Whitcomb embodying the "new" value system, Merriwell becomes convinced that Mormonism may not be so bad after all.

"We have pledged ourselves to Tom Whitcomb, and we'll stand by him through thick and thin." "Through thick and thin!" echoed Merriwell. "He seems to be a white man and all right, even if he is a Mormon." "Do you know, I am getting a different opinion of the Mormons than I once had." "How is that?" "Why, the Mormons I have seen seem like other people. I believe some of the wild stories told about their religion, and their ways are a mess of lies." The Mormons are not what they were, Jack. They have changed in recent years, and the younger Mormons are all right. They still hold to their religion, but they have cast aside polygamy, and I believe no man has a right to say how another shall worship God.

While the author was clearly not ready to abandon all the previous stereotypes, he was able to present a few new images. Juxtaposed to earlier Mormon stereotypes, these characters exhibited new qualities that supported the ideas that Mormons could be humane "like other people," that "wild stories" circulated about the Mormon religion, or that the Mormons were entitled to freedom of worship. It seemed as if national awareness of Mormonism was evolving. However a series of events quickly reestablished earlier stereotyping and halted changes in attitudes toward Mormonism for several years.

Politics and the Mormons, 1898–1907

When B. H. Roberts was elected to the House of Representatives in 1898 this hiatus came to an abrupt end. Recent accommodations that had paved the way for Utah's statehood were precarious, and Roberts' decision to run for Congress was probably unwise.[7] Roberts had practiced polygamy and was a leader in the Mormon church. When George Q. Cannon, also a church leader, had earlier served as territorial delegate, the propriety of merging state and church roles had been questioned. Subsequently, showing some sensitivity to church-state issues, Mormon leaders had provided that general authorities in the church obtain permission before running for political office. The election of B. H. Roberts again focused attention on the question of church and state separation.

Polygamy was even more capable of arousing public excitement. The Wilford Woodruff Manifesto of 1890 had officially ended plural marriage, and the constitution under which Utah became a state in 1896 forbade the practice; however, two problems lingered. Despite official assurances to the contrary, some new plural marriages continued to be contracted. These were few and eventually most were terminated, but evidence of the practice of polygamy was a source of on-going irritation to those who were suspicious of the Mormons. Also some Mormons who had contracted plural marriages before 1890 continued to live with their families as evidenced by children born to some plural wives.[8] Among the Mormons there were conflicting signals. Some leaders insisted that the law be obeyed in every particular, which would have disallowed any kind of maintenance of a plural marital relationship, even a formal, unphysical one.

7. For Roberts' own view of the issues see B. H. Roberts, *Comprehensive History of the Church of Jesus Christ of Latter-day Saints*, 6 vols. (Salt Lake City: Deseret Book Co., 1930), 6:363–74. For the basic details of the case see Davis Bitton, "The B. H. Roberts Case, 1898–1900," *Utah Historical Quarterly* 25 (1957): 27–46. Also see Truman G. Madsen, *Defender of the Faith* (Salt Lake City: Bookcraft, 1980).

8. For an analysis of the complexities of this issue see Kenneth L. Cannon II, "Beyond the Manifesto: Polygamous Cohabitation among LDS General Authorities after 1890," *Utah Historical Quarterly* 46 (Winter 1978): 24–36.

Others preached either publicly or privately that honor required continuing support for plural wives and cohabitation and the birth of children. Non-Mormon officials were not always in agreement either. Some demanded obedience to the law with no exceptions and no flexibility. Others, more sympathetic to the Mormons' plight, were willing to show restraint in prosecuting the technical infractions of cohabitation as long as no new plural marriages were contracted.[9]

Clearly the election to Congress of B. H. Roberts in 1898 presented great provocation since he was not only a general authority in the church, but maintained his marital relationship with three wives and the children from those marriages. To make matters worse, one of Roberts' plural wives gave birth to twins.

The newspapers had a field day. The *Detroit Journal* pictured Roberts carrying a set of twins followed by his three wives and an odd assortment of children.[10] On 22 November 1898 the *Salt Lake Tribune* showed Roberts unable to unlock the door of Congress with the key of polygamy. Charles Neland of the *New York Herald* depicted Roberts as a large reptile waddling up the steps of Congress.[11] Uncle Sam is only belatedly startled from his sleep. "Bart" of the *Minneapolis Tribune* of 19 December 1898 built on the theme of Roberts' entry into Washington by imagining him selecting a wife as traveling companion: "Monkey, monkey, barrel of beer, how many monkeys are there here? One, two three, out goes she" (Figs. 50, 51). Within the week the same newspaper reprinted a lengthy poem from the *Cleveland Leader* entitled: "When Roberts Gets to Washington."[12] Here is the last stanza.

> When Roberts gets to Washington
> With those three ladies who
> Are kept to sew his buttons on
> And nurse his babies too:
> Who build the furnace fires, and
> Who cook and bake and patch
> And when he whistles, take their stand
> And humbly toe the scratch
> A light may then be thrown upon
> The whole mysterious biz
> When Roberts gets to Washington
> With those three wives of his.

Fig. 50. "The Mormon Member from Utah." Reprinted in the *Salt Lake Tribune*, 25 December 1898, from the *Minneapolis Journal*.

Fig. 51. "Roberts's Rules of Order: It is to be Hoped They Will Not Supersede Reed's Rules in the Lower House of Congress." Reprinted in the *Salt Lake Tribune*, 25 November 1899, from the *Minneapolis Journal*.

9. These different approaches are well exemplified by the different witnesses and the majority and minority reports of the Smoot hearings, discussed below. Perhaps the best guide through the morass of the early 1890s is now Edward Leo Lyman, "The Mormon Quest for Utah Statehood" (Ph.D. dissertation, University of California at Riverside, 1981).

10. May was the artist of this *Detroit Journal* cartoon which appeared 17 November 1898.

11. *New York Herald*, 25 November 1898. The same cartoon was reprinted in the *Chicago Tribune*, 27 November 1898.

12. *Minneapolis Tribune*, 25 December 1898, reprinted from *Cleveland Leader*.

Fig. 52. "The Verdict." *Salt Lake Tribune*, 22 January 1900, reprinted from the *Syracuse Herald*.

On New Year's Day 1899, the *New York World* printed a signed dispatch from Lorenzo Snow, president of the church, denying any breach of faith. "The implied understanding with the nation when Utah entered the Union as a State has been sacredly observed," said Snow. He affirmed that plural marriages had ceased and that he had no intention of permitting additional polygamous marriages. He also appealed for understanding in behalf of those, like Roberts, who chose to remain as husbands and fathers to multiple families. "What were those men to do with their plural families?" asked the Mormon leader. "Cast them off? Repudiate their wives? Bastardize their children?"[13]

One cartoon in the *Salt Lake Tribune* of 27 September 1899 portrayed a perplexed Roberts in dialogue with the victim of the celebrated Dreyfus affair. Roberts wondered why he too could not be pardoned. "All you need is the public with you, and fewer wives," said Dreyfus.

Roberts presented himself for swearing in December 1898. There was an objection and the case was referred to a committee, which continued its protracted sessions through most of 1899. Toward the end of 1899 the Roberts case rapidly moved to conclusion. Most cartoons showed efforts to prevent Roberts from taking his seat.[14] "Vet," of the *Detroit Journal*, showed Uncle Sam and Roberts pushing on opposite sides of the Congressional door.[15] On 27 November 1899 Felix Mahoney of the *Washington Star* tied the boulder of polygamy to Roberts' back preventing him from entering Congress. The *Washington Post's* Berryman showed Roberts' path to the Capitol blocked by a mammoth pile of petitions on 28 November. The *Omaha News* and the *Washington Star* pulled the proverbial chair out from under a surprised Roberts.[16] R. C. Bowman, in the *Minneapolis Tribune* of 28 November, removed him from his chair aided by a thumbtack—"That point of order." "Bart" chose a revolving door to paint his plight in the *Minneapolis Journal* on 30 November 1899. No sooner did Roberts seem to be entering than he was on his way out again. On the same day the *St. Paul Pioneer Express*, inspired by the Thanksgiving season, dressed Roberts as a turkey ready for the kill.

On 2 December 1899 the *New York Journal* showed rolls of

13. Alongside the Lorenzo Snow dispatch, the *World* printed sensational stories which were included as a rebuttal of the Snow statement.

14. For a clever exception see *Minneapolis Journal*, 17 November 1899. This cartoon also appeared in the *Detroit Journal*, 20 November 1899.

15. *Detroit Journal*, 22 November 1899. The *Salt Lake Tribune* copied the same basic idea on 25 November 1899, but gave credit to the *New York World*.

16. *Omaha News*, reprinted in the *Salt Lake Tribune*, 27 November 1899. The *Washington Star* cartoon was also reprinted in the *Tribune* on 29 November 1899.

petitions being carried by train to Washington on the "Anti–Polygamy Special."[17] In one novel creation a gigantic woman, labeled polygamy, wrapped her arm around Roberts, while he said, "There's only one girl in the world for me."[18] Throughout the month of December cartoons continued to proliferate.[19]

On the first of January 1900 the *Washington Star* facetiously wished Roberts a "Happy New Year." Homer Davenport caricatured Roberts defending himself before Congress in the *New York Journal* on 6 January. When it became clear that the only division in the committee was over the question of how, not whether, Roberts would be kept out of Congress, cartoonists began to depict his inevitable departure. "Bart" envisioned his "escape from Washington via a helium balloon" in the *Minneapolis Journal* on 8 January. Davenport assigned female pall-bearers to carry the Roberts casket along the railroad tracks back home on 18 January in the *New York Journal*. In the *St. Paul Pioneer Press* on the twenty-first, Rehse depicted Roberts accepting Horace Greeley's advice from Uncle Sam to "Go West." The *Cleveland Plain Dealer* showed bipartisan Republican and Democratic overshoes kicking him out the Congressional door on the twenty-second. On the same day the *Minneapolis Journal* remonstrated: "A bad egg sure enough, but how about the hen that laid the egg?"

The majority of the committee advocated that Roberts be excluded from his seat while a minority said he should be seated and then expelled (Fig. 52). "Tis not a debate; Tis a funeral oration," said the caption under a Davenport cartoon in the *New York Journal* on 23 January 1900 depicting the lifeless body of Roberts. Roberts said in his farewell address, " I find myself in the position where one could say, with some propriety, perhaps, 'a plague on both your houses' [laughter], since the propositions of both minority and majority reports equally propose my undoing."[20] The majority report passed resoundingly, and Roberts returned to Utah (Fig. 53). During his farewell address he said, "You can brand me with shame and send me forth but I will leave with head erect and shall walk the earth as angels

Fig. 53. "How it Looked in November, 1898, and How it Looks Now. 'Ha! Ha! Ha! That's my Pa! He'll go to Washington, but won't take Ma.' 'Ha! Ha! Ha! Here comes Pa! Fired out of Washington, too much Ma!' " *Salt Lake Tribune*, 29 January 1900.

17. Cf. *Minneapolis Tribune*, 3 December 1899; *New York Journal*, 5 December 1899; *Minnesota Journal*, 5 December 1899; *Detroit Journal*, 5 December 1899.

18. *St. Paul Pioneer Press*, 5 December 1899.

19. *Denver Post*, 6 December 1899; *Washington Post*, 6 and 7 December 1899; *Minneapolis Tribune*, 7 December 1899; *St. Paul Pioneer Press*, 7 December 1899; *Denver Evening Post*, 8 December 1899; *Philadelphia Record*, 8 December 1899; *St. Louis Globe Democrat*, 10 December 1899; *New York Herald*, 11 December 1899; *Chicago Record*, 17 December 1899; *Minneapolis Journal*, 13 December 1899; *Washington Star*, 23 December 1899; *Denver Post*, 24 December 1899; *Minneapolis Tribune* from *Philadelphia Record*, 24 December 1899; *Washington Post*, 24 December 1899; *Salt Lake Tribune*, 27 December 1899; *Denver Post*, 24 December 1899.

20. As quoted in Bitton, "The B. H. Roberts Case," p. 44.

Fig. 54. "A Pleasant Surprise for the Girl Who
Marries a Utah Widower." *Life*, 4 May 1899.

walk with clouds."[21] In the *Minneapolis Tribune* of 29 January, cartoonist R. C. Bowman equipped Roberts with angel wings "to carry him back to Utah."

Some cartoons and newspaper articles took the position of the committee minority and questioned the constitutional legality of the exclusion.[22] Most newspaper articles simply justified Roberts' exclusion, offering the same grounds as those in the majority report. One argument, rejected of course by Roberts, was that his election had violated a compact or condition of statehood. In a Davenport cartoon in the *New York Journal* on 10 January 1900 Uncle Sam pointed to "Utah's Promise" as the cause for action. These and the other arguments of the committee majority were sufficiently convincing for most people.

During the months of the Roberts case only minor rumblings about the Mormons came from sources other than the newspapers. A handful of illustrations appeared in books and a few in periodicals.[23] *Life* featured two cartoons. The first, "A Pleas-

21. Ibid., p. 45.

22. Recent evaluations of the Roberts' case tend to agree with this view. See William Griffin White, Jr., "The Feminist Campaign for the Exclusion of Brigham Henry Roberts from the Fifty-Sixth Congress," *The Journal of the West* 17 (January 1978): 45–52. For the editorial position claiming exclusion represented a greater evil than the one the legislators sought to cure, see *New York Times*, 17 December 1899, p. 24. Cartoons identifying with this position can be found in the *New York World* by C. G. Bush reprinted in the *Salt Lake Herald*, 10 February 1900, and one by Lovey also in the *Salt Lake Herald*, 27 January 1900.

23. For book illustrations during this period see A. D. Gash, *The False Star* (Chicago: W. B. Conkey Company, 1899); J. H. De Wolff, *Pawnee*

ant Surprise for the Girl Who Marries a Utah Widower,"
appeared on 4 May 1899 and showed the widower introducing
his new spouse to an array of children and former wives (Fig.
54). The second appeared on 27 December 1900 as a flashback
to the 1847 Mormon migration across the plains. The cartoon
featured comical, stereotyped pioneers reading the Book of Mormon on horseback or preoccupied with diversions of courtship
along the trail.

In 1900–1901, several anti-Mormon cartoons appeared in
the *Salt Lake Tribune*.[24] However, little occurred on the national
horizon until the election of church apostle Reed Smoot to the
U.S. Senate in 1903. This provoked another *cause célèbre* that
became a cartoonist's delight for the next three years. Reed
Smoot's chances for acceptance in the Senate were better than
Roberts' since Smoot was monogamous and belonged to the
party in power, the Republicans. However, his position as a
church official raised some questions. Did he have the moral
qualifications to hold office? Would he act independently of his
ties with the church? Could Mormons be trusted to comply with
the laws of the land? Though Smoot was conditionally seated
as a member of the Senate, the committee on privileges con-
ducted a full-scale investigation.[25]

Although the committee hearing did not begin until 1904,
many anticipatory cartoons appeared locally throughout 1903.
Two newspapers in Salt Lake City, the *Tribune* and the *Herald*,
published many cartoons on Smoot. The *Tribune's* distinctly
anti-Mormon stand colored local attitudes; however, it was in
disseminating images to the national media that the *Tribune*
was most effective.

The *Salt Lake Herald*, while generally pro-Mormon, was not
the stronghold of partisanship some expected. Lovey, a non-
Mormon and the *Herald's* leading cartoonist, featured Smoot
and his problems in two dozen cartoons. When Teddy Roosevelt expressed dismay at Smoot's election, Lovey pictured Smoot

Bill (Pawnee Bill's Historic Wild West Company, 1902); Geraldine Bon-
ner, *Tomorrow's Tangle* (Indianapolis: Bobbs-Merrill Company, 1903),
illustrations by Arthur J. Keller; Harry Leon Wilson, *The Lions of the Lord*
(Boston: Lothrop, Lee and Shepherd Company); Charles Bertrand Lewis,
Bessie Baines or, The Mormon's Victim (Boston: Office of Ballou's Monthly
Magazine, Novellette No. 4, 1898). In Utah, two periodicals, *Lucifer's
Lantern* and the *Kinsman*, carried an occasional illustration. Nationally,
illustrated stories were not commonplace. See "Fanny Dare—A Utah Love
Story," illustrated by Miss A. Bradshaw, *The Overland Monthly* (June
1899), pp. 495–503.

24. *Salt Lake Tribune*, 1, 6 February; 11, 24 March; 22 June; 9 September 1900.

25. See *Proceedings Before the Committee on Privileges and Elections
of the United States Senate in the Matter of the Protests Against the Right
of Hon. Reed Smoot, a Senator from the State of Utah, to Hold His Seat*
4 vols. (Washington, D.C.: Government Printing Office, 1904–6).

Fig. 55. "What They Expected at Washington." From *Cartoons by Lovey*, published in 1907.

on 24 February 1903 reading "The Handwriting on the Walls" from TR: "You Had Better Stay Home." In one cartoon Lovey sketched "What They Expected at Washington" from the train bearing the Smoot entourage (Fig. 55).[26] The first railroad car carried husbands—antique males with their long beards hanging out the windows. Typically the next several cars were packed to the brim with wives. The remaining cars, as far as the eye could see, were for the children, some of whom, for want of room, sat on top of the train. Another cartoon portrayed the "welcome reception" in the nation's capital. Extending the right hand of fellowship, the greeters concealed weapons behind their backs with the other hand.[27] Another example, from the *Salt Lake Herald* on 6 March 1903, showed the new senator receiving "wild applause from the gallery," the ovation coming from a single member of Smoot's staff. Lovey's cartoons reflected the atmosphere of anticipation felt by the nation as the public hearing approached.

Nationally a cartoon in the *Washington Star* on 5 March 1904 publicized the "Standing Room Only" popularity of the proceedings. Showing disdain for the Mormons, "Bart," in the *Minneapolis Journal* on 4 March, clamped a clothespin on the nose of the United States Senate. Similarly the *Detroit Journal's* May on 5 March showed Uncle Sam proclaiming that the room where the "Mormon Family Wash" was done would need fumigating.

Perhaps the most important witness at the hearings was Mormon church president Joseph F. Smith, nephew of the founding prophet. He disavowed performing or authorizing polygamous marriages after 1890, but candidly acknowledged allegiance to plural wives and their children taken before the Woodruff Manifesto was issued.[28] Cartoonist "Bart's" inspiration for one draw-

26. *Cartoons by Lovey* (Salt Lake City: The Lovey Fund, 1907).

27. *Salt Lake Herald*, 24 February 1903.

28. Some post-manifesto marriages had been performed—mainly outside the boundaries of the United States. As this information came to light, the relationship of trust was strained once again. See Victor W. Jorgensen and B. Carmon Hardy, "The Taylor-Cowley Affair and the Watershed of Mormon History," *Utah Historical Quarterly* 48 (Winter 1980):4–36.

ing came from the size of Smith's family and a Mother Goose rhyme. (Fig. 56).[29]

> There was an old man who lived in a shoe
> He had so many children he didn't know what to do
> He couldn't keep count—they just grew and grew—
> And before he hardly knew it, he had forty-two.

After his testifying, the *Detroit Journal* featured President Smith "whitewashing" the Mormon temple with black paint on 9 March 1904. Nor did Smoot's stock soar. A cartoon in a Nashville newspaper concluded: "A man is known by the company he keeps."[30]

In December of 1904 another flurry of cartoons appeared across the nation. R. Sidney Smith of the *Pittsburgh Post* put Reed Smoot in a frying pan over coals of public indignation on 14 December 1904. In the same vein, Senator Burrows, chairman of the investigating committee, is shown counting stockings on the clothesline in Utah saying, "S-H-H-H! Here's where we get the proof."[31]

In Utah the *Salt Lake Herald* continued to feature Lovey's cartoons on Smoot. Lovey put Smoot in the Senate boxing ring waiting for separate pugilistic challenges from Senator Burrows and the ministerial association on 7 January 1904. On 26 February he cartooned the serving of subpoenas as "A Popular Spring Diversion in Utah." On 4 March after Joseph F. Smith testified, Lovey showed beads of perspiration rolling down Smoot's face, his hair standing straight on end. And he candidly captured the mutual ambivalence of Teddy Roosevelt and Smoot for each other in 1904.[32]

The works of other cartoonists printed in the *Salt Lake Herald* manifested a relatively impartial mood. They borrowed a cartoon on polygamy from the *Chicago Inter-Ocean* to represent the prevailing Mormon image in the media "if the reports from the Smoot investigation are to be believed."[33] A serial cartoon showed an old gentleman applying for multiple marriage licenses. Another *Herald* cartoon by Evans on 1 December 1904 lightly described the opposition of certain national women's organizations. Lining up women on both sides of the street to the Capitol (holding brooms, irons, rolling pins, and other formida-

Fig. 56. "Up-to-Date Father Goose." Drawn by Bart for the *Chicago Journal*, 9 March 1904.

29. Our records show this cartoon credited to the *Chicago Journal*, 9 March 1904, but we suspect since "Bart" drew for the *Minneapolis Journal* that the original drawing was published there.

30. Nashville, Tennessee, 12 March 1904. For other related cartoons see *American Affairs*, 17 March 1904; *New York World*, 10 March and 13 March 1904.

31. *Detroit Journal*, 28 December 1904.

32. *Salt Lake Herald*, 19 and 20 May 1904.

33. Ibid., 25 April 1904, reprinted from *Chicago Inter-Ocean*. See also *Salt Lake Herald*, 26 December 1904, for another example from the *Clevelan Plain Dealer*.

Fig. 57. "Portrait of a Latter Day Saint." Drawn by Charles Dana Gibson for *Colliers Weekly*, 26 March 1904.

ble instruments), he depicted "A warm reception in store for Senator Smoot." And again on 7 December another, captioned "The open season for witnesses," showed the marshal coming through one side of a revolving door and a witness exiting the other way.

After 1904, national newspaper cartooning of Smoot and the Mormons declined. The committee hearings had been concluded, even though the official report was not issued. Smoot was now seated and functioning in the U.S. Senate, where he would serve for almost thirty years. Furthermore, Mormon authorities issued a second manifesto declaring their intention to submit to the laws of the land, and two ecclesiastical leaders sympathetic to polygamy resigned from office.[34] Still, cartoons occasionally appeared in newspapers such as the *Pittsburgh Post*, *Chicago Inter-Ocean*, *Indianapolis Sentinel*, *Fort Wayne News*, *Washington Post*, and the *Burning Bush* from Waukesha, Wisconsin.[35]

As the long, drawn-out discussion over Smoot came to a close, the *Washington Herald* made a humorous point about the amount of time the decision was taking. Cartoonist Jack Smith pictured an aged Reed Smoot still waiting for a vote on the matter in 1950.[36] But early in 1907 the decision came when, by a narrow margin, the Senate rejected the committee's majority report and seated Smoot. The *Detroit Journal* on 22 February 1907 sketched the opposition to Smoot in the wreckage of an automobile alongside the "Senatorial Road." Facetiously Chairman Burrows remarked to Wm Alen "You're a peach of a chauffeur!"

From 1905 on the Utah-based *Salt Lake Tribune* produced anti-Mormon cartoons routinely. While Smoot was sometimes the subject, more than three hundred cartoons targeted church president Joseph F. Smith. His conservative appearance was frequently caricatured, and he often appeared in a butterfly bow tie, dark glasses, checked pants, striped cuffs, a top hat, and spats.[37] In many illustrations a battered halo dangles over his head. He was drawn as a spider, rat, elephant, turtle, and turkey or referred to as "profit." Joseph F. Smith became, as Brigham Young had, the focus for much of the hostility that was intended for the Mormon religion.

Magazines still treated Mormonism with comic flair. When Charles Dana Gibson was asked to supply the visual counterpart

34. James B. Allen and Glen M. Leonard, *The Story of the Latter-day Saints* (Salt Lake City: Deseret Book Co., 1976), pp. 444–74.

35. *Pittsburgh Post*, 30 January 1905; *Chicago Inter-Ocean*, 1 February 1905 and 4 June 1906; *Indianapolis Sentinel*, 9 January 1906; *Fort Wayne, Indiana, News*, 17 January 1906; *Washington Post*, 3 March and 31 March 1906; and *The Burning Bush*, Waukesha, Wisconsin, 29 March 1906.

36. *Washington Herald*, 28 January 1907.

37. For example, see *Salt Lake Tribune*, 16 May 1905.

Fig. 58. "Joseph Smith Comes to Washington." Drawn by F. T. Richards for *Life*, 31 March 1904.

to a scathing article on Mormonism in *Colliers*, the resulting caricature, "Portrait of a Latter Day Saint," stood incongruously against the acrimonious text by Alfred Henry Lewis (Fig. 57).[38] Whereas Lewis' words described the Mormons as vile and malicious, Gibson's illustration contained elements of pathos and sympathy. With certain exceptions, the image of the tragic figure or buffoon set the trend for most magazines illustrations through 1907. Of these magazines *Puck* and *Life* kept the Mormon visual image before the public more than any of the others.[39]

Except for a caricature of Joseph F. Smith coming to Washington to testify before the investigating committee on 31 March 1904, *Life* ignored the Smoot case (Fig. 58). Instead existing stereotypes entertained subscribers. On 21 April 1904, E. Frederick depicted contrasting perceptions of polygamy in *Life*. While a heavyset, plain wife reads from the newspaper "the horrors of Mormonism," her husband daydreams of three attractive wives. A week later C. F. Budd linked the Mormons with several other unpopular minorities. On 3 November 1904, another artist portrayed a Utah client asking his spiritualist medium for "the likeness of the woman I am going to marry." The medium replied, "I can give you a composite photograph." The fact that Mormons rejected spiritualist claims did not stop the association.

On 22 February, 1906, *Life's* Bayard Jones portrayed the Mormon husband's affectionate greeting: "One at a time, dears."[40] The women were tastefully drawn and believable types as opposed to the crude caricatures of Mormon women typical

---

38. *Colliers*, 26 March 1904. Gibson's temperament probably did not mesh with the bitterness in Lewis's article. The artist was most noted for the "Gibson girl"; many other illustrations of his held a kinship to the type of work that might have been expected from the pen of Norman Rockwell.

39. *Harper's Weekly*, for example, published just one cartoon on the Mormons after the turn of the century (7 May 1904). For examples from *Puck* for this period see Chapter 8.

40. *Life*, 22 February 1906.

Fig. 59. *"First Mormon*: 'How did that chorus girl you married turn out?' *Second Mormon*: 'Splendid. I'm now trying to make arrangements with the rest of the chorus.' " *Life*, 12 April 1906.

of earlier years. Another cartoon by Foster took the Mormon protagonists out of the customary rural setting and dressed them in tuxedos and top hats (Fig. 59). Breaking away from traditional stereotypes signified some marginal acceptance. Typically the accompanying dialogue referred to polygamy. *"First Mormon*: How did that chorus girl you married turn out? *Second Mormon* Splendid: I'm now trying to make arrangements with the rest of the chorus."[41]

From other sources this lighter tone cropped up. On 16 November 1905 a previously hostile *Judge* offered lines by Strickland W. Gillilan on "Santa in Salt Lake."

To a thrifty Mormon household came the patron saint of Yule;
He was puffing like an engine, he was laden like a mule.
For he knew a row of stockings such as nowhere else is seen
Would be yawning there before him in the home of Elder Green.
So he shoved his pack ahead of him and started down the flue,
While he muttered, 'This is something that I hate like smoke to do.'
Then he followed with reluctance through the smooty, smudgy air;
Quickly landing where the hosiery was hung in many a pair.

There were papa's socks and twenty pairs of lengthy, wifely hose;
There were socks for Eddie, Willie, for Eliphalet and Mose;
There were stockings of Matilda's, Esmeralda's and Susanne's,
There were Charley's hose and Molly's, Cora Belle's and little Dan's;
Amaryllis, George, Alphonso, Peter, Joseph, Maude, Eugene,
Arthur, Lizzie, James, Amelia, Mary, Frances, and Irene,
Briggie, Reed, Lucile, Clorinda, Arethusa, John, Estelle,
Mattie, Lucifer, Elfrida—from his lips their titles fell.

But about the shelf there dangled other hose whose owners' names
He could not recall to save him as he watched the dying flames.
Seven pairs, all baby sizes, each in age not quite a year—
'Gee!' cried Nick. 'Been something doing since the last time
   I was here.'
Glad I brought a stock of rattles and a lot of teething-rings—
Utah always gives a market for such kindergarten things.
From 'race suicide' she ever has discreetly held aloof,
And there's not a home in Zion free from stork-tracks on the roof.

While one cannot detect commendation in these verses or the cartoons from *Life*, neither is there much evidence of censure. The comic genre, which had served as a vessel of hostility for so many years, could also narrow the social distance between Mormons and other Americans.

Oversimplification of Mormonism in illustrations was dominant in the ten-year period from B. H. Roberts' election to Congress until Reed Smoot's eventual acceptance. Stereotyping might have been reduced had the Mormons adjusted and accommodated more rapidly to inevitable social changes. At the start of a new century, Americans were coming into greater contact with each other as transportation improved and communication

41. Ibid., 12 April 1906. Other cartoons were published 6 April 1905 and 22 November 1906.

systems developed. American culture had been characterized by individuality; with changes in the new century it would begin to move toward increased homogeneity. While many cartoonists created images based on the rich medium of humor and good-natured fun, some cartoons were still laced with varying degrees of hostility. Even as greater tolerance toward Mormonism evolved, at the start of the new century much of the humor in illustrations continued to be rooted in misinformation, exaggeration, and distortion.[42]

The Decline of National Attention, 1908–14

Seating Smoot did not create universal tolerance, but it did remove Mormonism from the foreground of public attention. During the next seven years newspapers rarely cartooned the Mormons. No cartoons appeared in *Puck*, and *Life* managed only four. Mormonism as a central theme in national cartoons was becoming rare.

Even the *Salt Lake Tribune* issued fewer cartoons on Mormonism. Over two hundred anti-Mormon drawings appeared in 1906, over a hundred in 1907, less than seventy in 1908 and 1909, less than thirty-five in 1910, and only a few in 1911. Those cartoons that did appear were far less hostile.

Among the few illustrations on Mormonism appearing prior to World War I were a caricature of Joseph F. Smith by R. F. McCardell, four cartoons from *Life*, and one from the English *Punch's Almanack* (Fig. 60). These were scattered between 1911 and 1914.[43] Cartoons that were more derogatory were published in *Pearson's Magazine* (1910), *Cosmopolitan* (1911), and in an anti-Mormon pamphlet (1910).[44] Internationally, a campaign against Mormonism in the British Isles spawned its

---

42. A softening of harsh imagery for other groups paralleled this general trend for Mormons. "One feature of Black efforts to gain dignity, acceptance, and recognition in the United States was the building of positive stereotypes to replace the negative ones. The evidence suggests that the coarseness and grossness typical of the 1880s and 1890s began to yield to more attractive and pleasant characterizations between 1900 and 1920. Of course, the ugly image did not disappear, but it did have new and vigorous competition. By 1920 one could see some definite improvement." J. Stanley Lemons, "Black Stereotypes as Reflected in Popular Culture, 1880–1920," *American Quarterly* 29 (Spring 1977):102–16.

43. *Morals and Immortals* (New York: Howeet Publishing Co., 1911) —the title page indicates that the caricatures were by C. De Fornaro, although the caricature was signed by R. L. McCardell; *Life*, 18 May 1911, 21 August 1913, 22 January 1914, and 25 June 1914; *Punch's Almanack*, 26 June 1912.

44. Richard Barry, "The Mormon Method in Business," *Pearson's Magazine* 24 (1910):571–78; Alfred Henry Lewis, "The Viper on the Hearth," *Cosmopolitan Magazine* 50 (March 1911):439–50; "The Trail of the Viper" (April 1911):693–703; "The Viper's Trail of Gold" (May 1911): 823–33; "The Peril of Mormonism" (Interdenominational Council of Women for Christian and Patriotic Service, 1910), pamphlet.

Fig 60. "The Mistletoe Tradition at Salt Lake City."
Punch's Almanack for 1912.

share of scurrilous prints, some of which were published in the *Liverpool Weekly Courier*.[45]

But the general picture was brighter. The virtual disappearance of cartoons from the media, the decline in critical publicity, the moderated stance of the *Salt Lake Tribune* and the developing respect for Reed Smoot combined to bring about changes. As much as any other single factor responsible for conciliation, however, was the realization by Mormon leaders that they, too, must take a greater initiative in winning public trust. The course of accommodation was incomplete by 1914, but it had come a long way since that early anti-Mormon print of 1834.

---

45. Winifred Graham, "Story of Mormonism," *Liverpool Weekly Courier*, 14 September, 21 September, 28 September 1912.

PART II

Image Themes

4. Troublesome Bedfellows: Mormons and Other Minorities

On 8 February 1879, a provocative color print appeared in *The Wasp* over the caption "Uncle Sam's Troublesome Bedfellows" (Fig. 61).[1] The cartoon alluded to five minorities—Mormons, Chinese, blacks, native Americans, and Irish—which, along with other ethnic groups, had proven problematical for a nation wrestling with the challenges of pluralism. In the illustration Uncle Sam's powerful foot had already kicked a bearded Mormon and pig-tailed Chinese out of his bed. A wild-eyed American Indian, a large-eared, Sambo-like black, and a sleepy, simianized Irishman seemed to be awaiting a similar fate. "By reason of the very marked peculiarities which they possess," rationalized *The Wasp*, ". . . if Uncle Sam has the right and might to kick out one class of people who are troubling him, it is just possible that he might extend that right to some others who are doing their best to make themselves a nuisance."[2] While American political theory enunciated humanitarian and cosmopolitan ideas, welcoming "your tired, your poor . . . yearning to breathe free," the national record on the treatment of minorities left much to be desired.[3]

Although the title word "Wasp" in this San Francisco-based weekly referred to the insect with the robust sting, emblematic of the potency of the satirical magazine, it might just as well have stood for its more contemporary referent: white, Anglo-Saxon, Protestant. From the colonial era on these attributes tended to define the ground rules for social distance in the minds of many Americans. To the extent that any group deviated from these mainstream characteristics, they often fell heir to derision ranging from mild epithet to physical abuse. Racial deviation ordinarily brought the harshest condemnation, but national and religious differences also opened the floodgates of intolerance. Moreover, when two or more of these dimensions came together, as so often happened in the case of Irish-Catholics, Eastern European Jews, Mormon immigrants, transplanted African blacks,

---

1. *The Wasp*, 8 February 1879, p. 411.

2. Ibid., 8 February 1879, p. 435.

3. On the large question of immigration and the gap between idealistic expectations and the reality, see, for example, Ray Allen Billington, *The Protestant Crusade, 1800–1860* (Gloucester, Mass.: Peter Smith, 1963); John Higham, *Strangers in the Land* (New Brunswick, N.J.: Rutgers University Press, 1955); the various works by Oscar Handlin; and J. R. Pole, *The Pursuit of Equality in American History* (Berkeley: University of California Press, 1978). A thoughtful recent study that sees "a fundamental tension between pluralism and democracy" is Stephen Steinburg, *The Ethnic Myth* (1981).

or even more complex configurations of race, national origin, and religion, some degree of animosity seemed inevitable.[4]

Since diverse ethnic groups represented persistent problems for the nation, it is no wonder that minorities were compared, combined, and contrasted for effect.[5] Seldom was the stature of any one minority group enhanced by its association in the press with another. Rather, the negative impressions of blacks, for example, tarnished by association the image of the Irish and vice versa. "I remain convinced," write the historian Winthrop Jordan, "that white American attitudes toward blacks have done a great deal to shape and condition American responses to other racial minorities."[6] Representations of minorities in American image histories must be seen against the backdrop of earlier and contemporary images of the whole gamut of racial, national, or religious social groups. When Mormons were accused of not acting like "white men," when anti-Masonic, anti-Catholic, and anti-Mormon impressions blurred the distinctions between these groups,[7] when colonization proposals for Mormons resembled removal schemes for others,[8] when stereotypes labeling blacks were applied to other ethnic images,[9] when restrictive immigration proposals aimed against the Chinese seemed a good idea for application against the Mormons,[10] when the hot irons of Know-Nothingism branded more than Catholicism in the

4. Newly arrived African slaves or Chinese immigrants were condemned on three counts: race, foreign birth, and their "heathen" status.

5. The comparisons took on interesting coloration. For example, Southerners "suggested that Negroes are better off than Irish, citing the blight of the Northern Irish ghetto as evidence for the benefits of paternalistic slavery." See Stephen Garrett Bolger, *The Irish Character in American Fiction, 1830–1860* (New York: Ocno Press, 1976), pp. 110–11.

6. Winthrop D. Jordan, *The White Man's Burden* (New York: Oxford University Press, 1974), p. viii.

7. See David Brion Davis, "Some Themes of Counter-Subversion: An Analysis of Anti-Masonic, Anti-Catholic, and Anti-Mormon Literature," *The Mississippi Valley Historical Review* 42 (September 1960): 205–24.

8. Colonization campaigns "for ridding the state (and the entire nation) of black people" began in Virginia in the 1790s. Jordan, *The White Man's Burden*, pp. 205–6. *Harper's Weekly* indulged in wishful thinking by idealizing South America as a natural gathering place for Mormons. "South America contains thousands of square leagues of unoccupied territory, blessed with a glorious climate and a fertile soil, where no government would molest, no soldiers attack them, and where they might work out their problem in safety for at least a century to come." *Harper's Weekly*, 28 November 1857, p. 754. Later rumors had the Mormons on their way to Oceania. "A new programme for the Mormons is indicated. It is now proposed that they shall emigrate to one of the East India islands, and reliable information is said to have been received that they will do so." *Harper's Weekly*, 21 July 1860, pp. 454–55. The reliable information proved unreliable. See *Harper's Weekly*, 28 July 1860, pp. 470–71.

9. For a comparison between Irish and black stereotypes see John J. Appel, "From Shanties to Lace Curtains: The Irish Image in *Puck*, 1876–1910," *Comparative Studies in Society and History* 13 (October 1971): 365–76.

10. *The Argonaut*, 17 October 1885, pp. 1–2.

1850s,[11] the interconnection of ethnic imagery becomes abundantly evident.

This chapter will consider the blending of ethnic imagery between Mormons and other minorities in mass-produced prints. First to be considered will be those prints that included Mormons among several other minorities with the apparent intent of expressing the view that all such groups threatened the American way of life. Another set of illustrations described the Mormon family as consisting of diverse ethnic groups and assorted "ne'er-do-wells." Finally, the specific groups most frequently linked to Mormons in prints—Irish, Catholics, blacks, Chinese, native Americans—are examined and consideration is given to the ingenious ways in which the linkages were made plausible.

Several prints, like the initial example from *The Wasp*, simply fostered the conception of racial, national, or religious minorities as a thorn in the side of the nation. Mormons were not particularly singled out, but neither were they ignored. Additional prints from *The Wasp* maintained this tradition. "The Three Troublesome Children," designed by Frederick Keller, pictured an Indian child suggestively using a tomahawk to destroy U.S. toy soldiers while unruly Chinese and Mormon children pull on the matronly Columbia's hair and otherwise abuse her (Fig. 62).[12] Meanwhile, Uncle Sam, oblivious to the Mormon, Indian, and Chinese questions, turns his back to the fray and reads a newspaper headlined "politics." Another print perpetuated the "troublesome" theme with the caption "Uncle Sam's Troublesome School" (Fig. 63).[13] As the Republican and Democratic parties (an ape-faced Irish child represents the Democratic party) contend in the foreground, labor, and capital fight under Uncle Sam's nose. An Indian, faithful to the stereotype, stealthily slinks about as his tribal brothers attach a string of firecrackers to the beleaguered teacher's coattail. A person personifying California figuratively shuts the door before the Chinese schoolchild can enter, and Uncle Sam clings to the coat of a Mormon who, menacingly, holds three children in his clutches.

Not to be outdone, illustrated weeklies in the East, like *Puck*, also took a shotgun approach to minorities, compressing several into a single print. The particular mix of ethnicity sometimes differed; the Jewish image, for example, recurred more often in the East. But the message remained the same.

Puck's Frederick Opper spoofs a pretentious lineup of aspiring ethnic authors (Mormon, Jew, Irish, Chinese, European, and black) who wait entry into the office of *Century* magazine's

11. See John Higham, *Strangers in the Land: Patterns of American Nativism, 1860–1925* (New York: Atheneum, 1973), pp. 6–7.

12. *The Wasp*, 16 December 1881, p. 385.

13. Ibid., 5 June 1886, p. 16.

editor.[14] (The occasion for the cartoon was the magazine's generous payment to former President Ulysses S. Grant for his Civil War memoirs.) The titles of the manuscripts held by the prospective authors sustained the negative impressions: "I Led the Retreat at Bull Run" (Mormon), "Quick Time at Bull Run" (Irish), " 'Washing Through the War'—by General Shirts" (Chinese), "The Dark Side of the Late War" (black), and "Rebellion and Lager Bier" (German). Just one week later the Jewish Shylock image, bearing the label bankruptcy, appeared with a Mormon, among others, personifying a picture of duplicity and exploitation.[15] Both the Jew and the Mormon were seen as foes blocking Grover Cleveland's pathway to the White House. Earlier, a print from the short-lived *American Punch* contrasted "the pure of all the earth" with Catholicism, Mormonism, Judaism, Spiritism, Boss Tweed, Clerical Fraud, Chinese, and blacks, noting that such "shall one day feel the dread avenging angel's lightning thrust."[16]

Grappling with the sensitive issue of intercultural marriage, some cartoonists maligned Mormons by portraying the Mormon family as the domicile for ethnic intermixing. C. F. Budd's lively artistic rendition in *Life* is the best example of this approach (Fig. 65).[17] Nine six-year olds, "who take after their mothers," are displayed out on a walk with their Mormon father. Scottish, native American, Oriental, Dutch, black, Jewish, and other ethnic groups are depicted as family members.[18] Even more prevalent were nativist-inspired prints accusing Mormons of converting a disproportionate number of European women proselytes to meet the institutional demands of polygamy. Immigration statistics failed to support the myth, but prejudice kept these suspicions alive.[19] One impassioned, emotional appeal from *Frank Leslie's Illustrated Newspaper* pictured immigrant women from many lands of Europe carrying "sealed" signs connoting a predetermined marital destiny even before their arrival in Utah (Fig. 66).[20] Each symbolically enters the Salt Lake Valley through the jaws of an enormous, foreboding skull containing armed male overseers in the eye sockets. Another portrayed a

14. *Puck*, 11 February 1885.

15. *Puck*, 18 February 1885.

16. *American Punch*, September 1879, pp. 102–3.

17. *Life*, 28 April 1904, p. 404.

18. For an earlier version of the same idea in print form see Fig. 112. Harry Scratchly designed the cartoon.

19. "All prevalent notions to the contrary, these converts . . . by and large embraced Mormonism in families. Lurid stories of abduction to supply women for Utah's supposed harems had their germ in occasional runaways and desertions, but the statistics and the accounts of the converts themselves provide a convincing, not to say startling, corrective of folklore," William Mulder, *Homeward to Zion* (Minneapolis: University of Minnesota Press, 1957), p. 107. For statistical comparisons see Mulder, p. 109.

20. *Frank Leslie's Illustrated Newspaper*, 4 February 1882, p. 409.

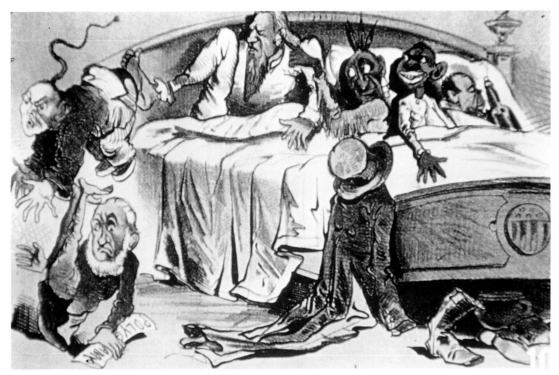

Fig. 61. "Uncle Sam's Troublesome Bedfellows." *The Wasp*,
8 February 1879.

Fig. 62. "The Three Troublesome Children." Drawn
by Keller for *The Wasp*, 16 December 1881.

Fig. 63. "Uncle Sam's Troublesome School." Drawn by Walter for *The Wasp*, 5 June 1886.

Fig. 64. "Mormon Fishing in Foreign Lands." *The Wasp*, 27 November 1886.

Fig. 65. "Mormon Elder-berry—Out with His Six-Year-Olds, Who Take after Their Mothers." *Life*, 28 April 1904.

group of Scandinavian women at Castle Garden en route for Salt Lake City under the direction of Mormon missionaries (Fig. 67).[21] The women, labeled "lambs" in the caption, appeared apprehensive, sullen, and depressed, while the "wolves," the Mormon males, displayed obvious satisfaction with the catch. In a similar vein Thomas Nast decorated *Harper's Weekly* with Mormon males herding reluctant women down the gangplank as they disembark from an immigrant vessel.[22] As a final example from this tradition, *The Wasp*, assisted by color lithography, showed a Mormon missionary in red, white, and blue perched comfortably astride the American eagle in flight over Europe fishing for female proselytes from one end of the continent to another (Fig. 64).[23] American ethnocentrism, resentment against Mormonism, and a solution to the Mormon question were spelled out in the accompanying textual explanation:

> Were it not for international courtesy the Mormon would find it hard work to sustain his harems. He never could keep them up from American recruits. It is in foreign lands that he finds his fishing grounds. There only do the suckers bite. Safely ensconced behind his credentials as a free American citizen he casts his intriguing lines amid the abodes of the oppressed, the lowly and the poor abroad, and entices them to his hook by the bait of alluring promise of independence and comfort and final heaven. He beats all other missionaries in that he adds worldly happiness, practical home comfort here on earth to his other guarantee of celestial bliss. But the point we make is that it is the American eagle which gives him his poise and vantage ground. If our Government could withdraw this panoply of protection the business of recruiting inmates for the seraglios of Utah would soon come to an end.[24]

That this fairly complex verbal editorial could be compressed into a single illustration is a good example of the power of the pictorial approach.

---

21. Ibid., 15 December 1883, pp. 264–65.
22. Fig. 107, *Harper's Weekly*, 25 March 1882, p. 191.
23. *The Wasp*, 27 November 1886, cover.
24. Ibid., 27 November 1886, p. 3.

Fig. 66. "Mormonism in Utah—The Cave of Despair."
Frank Leslie's Illustrated Newspaper, 4 February 1882.

Competing with these ethnic images disparaging the Mormons by general ethnic associations were efforts to link Mormonism with specific minorities. Among these was the unlikely combination of Catholicism and Mormonism.

Mormons, Catholics, and the Irish

Although Catholicism and Mormonism are almost never thought of as similar, time and again they were mentioned in the same breath as twin menaces to American institutions. In a litany ritually recited by critics, both faiths were charged with: (1) deliberately subverting American values; (2) posing a threat to the constitutional principle of separation of church and state; (3) submitting to autocratic control from Rome and Salt Lake City—the latter labeled "A Yankee Vatican" in the pages of the English humor periodical *Punch*;[25] (4) sponsoring secret ceremonies of dubious repute; and (5) encouraging the licentious or economic exploitation of women.

Some works were so similar in tone that they seemed part of the same campaign. *Startling Disclosures of the Great Mormon Conspiracy Against the Liberties of this Country*[26] would have reminded readers of such sensational publications as *Awful Disclosures of the Hotel Dieu Convent of Montreal* or the *Secrets of Black Nunnery Revealed*.[27] These examples of scurrilous yellow journalism disclosed conspiracy motives, described lurid scenes, claimed the victimization of women, exposed unconventional religious rituals, and made up with livid color what they lacked in truth.

Other works explicitly brought the two religions together in order to slur them. Periodicals redolent with anti-Catholic content—*Thistleton's Illustrated Jolly Giant*, *Punch*, or *The Argonaut*—occasionally used anti-Mormon material as a weapon to slur Catholicism. Some anti-Mormon literature employed the same tactic. Such associations often stretched both the truth and the imagination. *Thistleton's Illustrated Jolly Giant* featured on the cover a Mormon participant in the Mountain Meadows

---

25. *Punch*, 16 May 1857, p. 194.

26. I. M'Gee Van Dusen and Maria Van Dusen [Van Deusen], *Startling Disclosures of the Great Mormon Conspiracy Against the Liberties of This Country* . . . (New York: Blake and Jackson, 1849).

27. Maria Monk, *Awful Disclosures of the Hotel Dieu Convent of Montreal, or the Secrets of Black Nunnery Revealed* (New York: 1836). For an historical analysis of Monk's book see Ray Allen Billington, *The Origin of Nativism in the United States, 1800–1844* (1933; repr. New York: Arno Press, 1974); and Maria Monk, *Awful Disclosures of the Hotel Dieu Nunnery* (Hamden, Conn.: Archon Books, 1962), with an introduction by Ray Allen Billington. Facsimile of 1836 edition. More than 300 thousand copies of Maria Monk's book were circulated by the Civil War. Richardson Wright, *Forgotten Ladies* (Philadelphia: n.p., 1928), pp. 142–43.

Fig. 67. " 'The Twin Relic of Barbarism.'—The Wolves and the Lambs—Arrival of Scandinavian Converts in Charge of Mormon Missionaries, at Castle Garden, en Route for Salt Lake City." *Frank Leslie's Illustrated Newspaper*, 15 December 1883.

Massacre, John D. Lee.[28] "My mother was a Catholic, and I was christened in the faith," noted the caption under Lee's picture, as if his remotest religious roots predisposed subsequent behavior. While the magazine did not absolve Mormon participants in the episode, it grasped at straws to implicate Catholicism. Slightly less anti-Mormon than anti-Catholic, *The Argonaut* took the percentage of increase of Mormon adherents between 1860 and 1884 to challenge the argument of rate of growth as a true test of religion. Mormonism's "percentage of increase in America . . . has been greater than that of the Roman Catholic church," reasoned *The Argonaut,* "so that by the percentage test between the papal and the Mormon churches the polygamous monstrosity of the Latter-day Saints is 'the only holy apostolic church.' "[29] While not a compliment to Mormonism, the statement was mainly intended as a derisive blow against Catholicism. Varying the method slightly, *Punch* simultaneously discredited Mormonism and Catholicism by comparing their centralized authority structures: "Brigham Young is a Pope in his way and his disciples and subjects are papists in theirs. Utah is an imperium in imperio, or at least an imperium in republica. But so is every Roman Catholic diocese."[30] Reporting on Horace Greeley's notable interview with Brigham Young for *Harper's Weekly,* *Punch* called the colorful Mormon leader the "Archhumbug," and humorously expressed preference for the "Pope of Utah's" interpretation of Paul's teaching that a bishop should be "the husband of one wife" *at least* as opposed to the Catholic inter-

28. *Thistleton's Illustrated Jolly Giant,* 24 March 1844, cover. For an analysis of American anti-Catholic caricature prints see John and Selma Appel, "The Grand Old Sport of Hating Catholics," *The Critic,* November–December 1971, pp. 50–58.

29. *The Argonaut,* 5 July 1884.

30. *Punch,* 16 January 1858, p. 30.

Fig. 68. "It Has Been Revealed to Me that I Should Marry You." Illustration from the German edition of Maria Ward's *Female Life Among the Mormons* published in 1857.

pretation that he should *have none at all.*[31] Although Catholicism suffered most from such comparisons, no gain in public image accrued to Mormonism.

In explicitly anti-Mormon publications Mormonism was assaulted with the battering ram of Catholic associations. Since mainstream Protestants were often behind both anti-Mormon and anti-Catholic crusades, they could enjoy ridiculing both religious rivals. One defamatory method was to clothe Mormons in the religious vestments of Catholicism. As early as 1842, F. E. Worcester, the engraver for John C. Bennett's anti-Mormon exposé, put Catholic bishop's mitres on the heads of Mormon leaders in each of three wood engravings.[32] Other elements of the prints suggested questionable secret ceremonies going on among the Mormons as with the Catholics. Worcester probably took his cue from Bennett's textual proclivity to apply the language of Catholicism—"Bull from His Holiness," "Mormon College of Apostles," "Mormon Pontiff"—to the Mormon condition. By the same token, the illustrated German and Swedish translations of Maria Ward's fanciful anti-Mormon novel *Female Life Among the Mormons* clothed Brigham Young in the robes of the Roman church (Fig. 68).[33] The Mormon prophet appears to be holding the handle of a knife concealed beneath his clothing as he exclaims authoritatively to a perplexed young woman, "It Has Been Revealed to Me that I Should Marry You." The autocratic, exploitative stereotypes of Catholicism were transferred to the Mormon setting, and both religions suffered in the process.

Thomas Nast, implacable foe of both Mormonism and Catholicism, approached these issues with a gravity uncharacteristic of cartoonists. On the whole, he treated Catholic and Mormon motifs separately and damned the two belief systems with equal fervor. Biographers have noted his anti-Catholic bias, but overlooked his penchant for branding Mormonism.[34] His perception of both religions as "foreign" threats to national liberty was visually represented by a Mormon turtle and Catholic alligator crawling over the dome of the Capitol of the United States

---

31. Ibid., 17 September 1859, p. 122.

32. John C. Bennett, *The History of the Saints* (Boston: Leland and Whiting, 1842), Chapter 1, note 18 and George C. Groce and David H. Wallace, *The New-York Historical Society's Dictionary of Artists in America, 1564–1860* (New Haven: Yale University Press, 1957), p. 114. Also see Sinclair Hamilton, *Early American Book Illustrators and Wood Engravers 1670–1870*, 2 vols. (Princeton: Princeton University Library, 1958), 1:88.

33. Maria Ward, *Mormonengräuel dargelegt in den Erlebnissen einer aus Utah Entflohenen Mormonenfrau* (Weimar, Germany: Gauss Verlag, 1857), facing 202. Maria Ward, *Qvinnan Bland Mormonerna* (Stockholm, Sweden: Schuck and Josephson, 1857).

34. Between 1881 and 1886 Nast created several cartoons on the Mormons for *Harper's Weekly.*

Fig. 69. "Religious Liberty is Guaranteed but Can We Allow Foreign Reptiles to Crawl Over US?" Drawing by Thomas Nast in the 1870s.

(Fig. 69).[35] Such treatment rivaled the tactics from the Know-Nothingism of an earlier era, the American Protective Association, or comparable anti-Mormon organizations.[36]

Since almost all Irish in America were Catholic, Irish and Catholic images tended to fuse. Mark Twain's *Roughing It* gives an example. Twain skillfully manipulated the Irish servant girl image to criticize the Mormons. If anyone could break into the distant inner circle of Mormons, reasoned Twain, it was the self-reliant, domineering, unpredictable, occasionally unscrupulous Irish Catholic maid. Wrote Twain:

> The hired girl of one of the American families was Irish, and a Catholic; yet it was noted with surprise that she was the only person outside of the Mormon ring who could get favors from the Mormons. She asked kindnesses of them often, and always got them. It was a mystery to everybody. But one day as she was passing out at the door, a large bowie-knife dropped from under her apron, and when her mistress asked for an explanation she observed that she was going out to 'borry a washtub from the Mormons'![37]

If the Bridget of Irish maid fame was not borrowing wash-tubs, she was throwing them at her henpecked, subjugated husband. *The Judge* snickered at women, Mormons, and the Irish through the cartoon medium.[38] Hardly any other mode of expression could match the cartoon for economy of meaning in saying so much. Just a few well placed lines lampooned the legendary wrath of women—"one wife enough for him"—

35. Whether this illustration appeared as a separately published print or elsewhere is unknown to the authors. We located the photograph of the print in the print collection at the Library of Congress.

36. The Women's National Anti-Polygamy Society represented the type of organization formed to deal with Mormonism.

37. Mark Twain, *Roughing It* (New York: Harper and Row, 1899), pp. 175–76.

38. *The Judge*, 27 October 1903, p. 6. See Appel, "From Shanties to Lace Curtains," pp. 365–75, for an analysis of the development of the Irish image.

Fig. 70. "Our Guardians: *First Irishman.*—It's all pinsion, pinsion, nowadays, Moike. The paper says, there's a thousand survivors of the Mexican War, with twelve thousand widdies, afther drawin' pinsions this blessed day!' *Second Irishman.*—'The owld Mormons! Twelve widdies to ivery one o' them! That's pfwhat becomes uv the surplush!' " *Puck*, 2 May 1888, drawn by Dalrymple.

Irish national character, and the plight of being a Mormon male in the presence of so many from the opposite sex. The customary simian physiognomy, the ramshackle shack, the slum-like surroundings, the pigs and goats on the premises rounded out the imagery of what it was thought to mean to be Irish.

An illustrated article on Mormon immigrants arriving at Castle Garden used the stereotypic image of Irish women to speculate on the forces behind the conversion of an Irish family to Mormonism. Describing the mother as the "presiding matron, a stout, severe Irishwoman," an immigrant official observes: "These are the first Irish Mormons that have ever passed through here; and it was the woman . . . who converted her husband; and she's the strongest kind of a convert, I tell you!"[39]

Dalrymple, a cartoonist for *Puck*, exploited Mormonism as a foil to expose the Irish intellect (Fig. 70).[40] Two Irish bachelors lament the absorption into Mormonism of twelve thousand widows from the "Mexican War." "The owld Mormons! Twelve widdies to ivery one o' them! That's pfwhat becomes uv the surplush!"

Mormons and Black Americans

Since black Americans were generally accorded the bottom rung of the ladder for minorities, placing other disliked groups on the same footing represented the ultimate insult to insensitive Americans. Tying Mormons to that deeply anchored social standing did nothing to elevate the impression of blacks. "The Lord intends that WHITE FOLKS, and not Mormons shall possess that goodly land" (Missouri), said one Mormon baiter.[41] Visually, the *New York Journal* portrayed Mormon aspirant to Congress B. H. Roberts "in the Bosom of His Admirers," including, of course, a black follower.[42] There were other variations on the same theme.[43]

Sometimes there was a more specific method to such madness. For example, from the earliest English perceptions of Africans evolved a belief in a "peculiarly potent sexuality."[44] By the

39. *Leslie's Weekly*, 23 November 1878, p. 208.

40. *Puck*, 2 May 1888, p. 168.

41. Bennett, *History of the Saints*, p. 193. This was relatively common discourse. "He seems to be a white man . . . even if he is a Mormon." By the author of Frank Merriwell, "Frank Merriwell Among the Mormons or The Lost Tribe of Israel," *Tip Top Weekly* 1 (June 19, 1897): 9.

42. *New York Journal*, 24 January 1900, sketch by Davenport.

43. Earlier we alluded briefly to colonization proposals generally reserved for blacks but occasionally applied to other groups like the Mormons. Even lynching was suggested as a method to consider for Mormons "when the blackmen are all lynched." *The Judge*, 17 June 1899, p. 370.

44. Jordan, *The White Man's Burden*, p. 25.

ninetenth century this belief was rampant in America.[45] When the Mormons announced the practice of polygamy in 1852, opportunists could not resist building a bridge between the libidinous imagery of blacks and Mormons. From the 1850s into the twentieth century illustrators employed the comparison.[46] Assailing Mormons seemed to be the major motive behind such illustrations. In a few cases it was impossible to identify the primary target, whether black or Mormon. It did not really matter, as both groups took their lumps.

Black Americans did not come through the back door as servants in most of this imagery. In several illustrations blacks appeared in a polygamous Mormon family, usually as one of the wives or as children. The national anxiety over miscegenation intensified the negative reaction. A cartoon in *Frank Leslie's Budget of Fun* showed Brigham Young deprived of his family as he is taken off to the U.S. court for trial. First in line at the "Affecting Parting of Brigham Young From his Interesting Little Family" is a black wife.[47] Elsewhere in the short-lived *Chic*, a black baby wails out a distress signal with eight other infants as some of their mothers wage a royal family battle in a color lithograph satirically entitled "The Elders' Happy Home" (Fig. 71)[48] In still another scene, this time from the melodramatic publication *The Mysteries of Mormonism*, sponsored by the *National Police Gazette*, "A 'Cullud' Mormon" raises eyebrows as he links arms affectionately with his white, female companion.[49] None of this visual association eased the accommodation of Mormons and blacks to the host culture.

Part of the unfortunate legacy from American popular culture is "Coon songs."[50] They held up black American to ridicule. Now and then other groups shared the scorn. One song, bearing the title "The Mormon Coon," exploited both groups and doubtless hoped to cash in on the popular song market (Fig. 72).[51] Confirming the stereotypes of amorous propensities among Mormons and blacks, the lyrics recited a story of a black

45. For a discussion of the functional utility of stereotypes towards blacks see Arnold Rose, *The Negro in America* (New York: Harper Torchbooks, 1964), pp. 39–41.

46. One of the earliest illustrations of a black Mormon appeared in *Nick Nax*, June 1858, p. 46. The clear intent obvious in the print was in maligning Mormons by their association with blacks.

47. *Frank Leslie's Budget of Fun*, January 1872, p. 16.

48. *Chic*, 19 April 1881, pp. 8–9.

49. See Chapter 2, note 62.

50. See J. Stanley Lemons, "Black Stereotypes as Reflected in Popular Culture, 1880–1920," *American Quarterly* 29 (Spring 1977), pp. 102–16, and Russell Nye, *The Unembarrassed Muse* (New York: The Dial Press, 1970), p. 317, for the impact of "Coon Songs."

51. Raymond A. Browne and Henry Clay Smith, "The Mormon Coon" (New York: Sol Bloom, 1905), Music Collection, Brown University.

traveling to Utah in the quest of plural romance. A sample of the verses follows:

I used to rave about a single life,
Now every day I get a brand new wife.

There's one gal I ain't married yet, but say,
I'm saving her up for a rainy day.

If you ain't never heard a cyclone roar,
Come up and hear just how my wives can snore.

It keeps me hustling in the loving line,
They all yell out, "I saw him first, he's mine."

I've got so many, I forget a lot,
I keep the marriage license door bell hot.

If on the street into a wife I run,
I have to ask her, "What's your number, Hon?"

The impossibilities of remembering the names of so many wives and the snoring problem, hackneyed by the beginning of the twentieth century, were refurbished for the benefit of "The Mormon Coon." The chuckles and guffaws issuing forth from the mirthful participants might well have been lost on Mormons and blacks.

A few years later the well-known black editor of the *New York Age*, Booker T. Washington, traveled to Utah. Painfully aware of the prejudice against his own people, he surmised that the popular reports about Mormons disseminated by the press might be equally suspect. Believing that "no person . . . can ever really know that race or that group of people until he gets into their homes," Washington wanted to draw his own conclusions. "There are many people today who consider themselves wise on the condition of the Negro who . . . know little about the moral standards and activities of the colored people. The same I am convinced is true regarding the Mormons. The people who speak in the most disrespectful terms . . . are those who know least about them."[52]

Mormons and Chinese

The pairing of Catholicism and Mormonism, or Irish or blacks and Mormons differed in substance and motivation. There were also unique elements underlying the Chinese-Mormon connection in the media. Of course, most of the anti-Chinese agitation came from the West Coast, where regional prejudice toward "John Chinaman" found its most virulent expression. Western weeklies like *The Wasp* and *The Argonaut* reported on the vexing Chinese question. Here the most influential lobby made its case for restrictive immigration of Asians. At the same time newspapers and illustrated weeklies chronicled the latest devel-

---

52. *New York Age*, 17 April 1913.

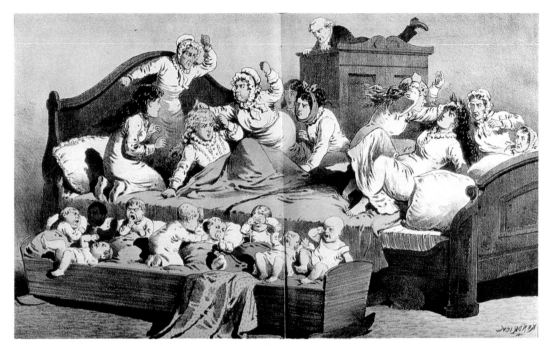

Fig. 71. "The Elders' Happy Home." *Chic*, 19 April 1881.

Fig. 72. "The Mormon Coon." Published by Sol Bloom in 1905.

Fig. 73. "Uncle Sam's Nightmare." From *The Wasp*, 24 March 1882, drawn by Keller.

Fig. 74. " 'The Chinese May Stay but the Mormons Must Go.'— De Witt Talmage." Drawn by Hamilton for *The Judge*, 27 October 1883.

opments on the Mormon question. The temporal and spatial contiguity of the Mormon and Chinese problems inevitably connected the two in the western press.[53] As a matter of fact, both the Edmunds Act against polygamy and the initial Chinese exclusion act were enacted by the same Congress in 1882. Subsequent legislation against the interests of Mormons and Chinese was enacted later in the same decade.

Generally speaking, both were simply treated as parallel problems in the press. During the years from 1879 to 1887 color prints containing Mormons and Chinese, often with other groups, appeared in *The Wasp*. The following are some of the variations: "Troublesome Bedfellows" (Fig. 61);[54] uninvited guests in the United States;[55] expendable trees needing to be cut down by presidential axe, like the fallen slavery tree;[56] along with the Indians, "The Three Troublesome Children" (Fig. 62);[57] two fat pigs next to an Indian rattlesnake as the illustrated weeklies ignore their presence by taking a "siesta"[58]; as "Uncle Sam's Nightmare," symbolized effectively by a Chinese-faced anchor and Mormon goat resting weightily on the body of a restless Uncle Sam (Fig. 73);[59] as members of "Uncle Sam's Troublesome School" (Fig. 63);[60] and as foreign refuse deposited on the "World's Dumping Ground"—America.[61] From the East, *The Judge* fused two popular impressions of Mormons and Chinese, the prolific Mormon family and the Chinese laundry. Eight pig-tailed employees of the "Sling Wah Chinese Laundry" carry the enormous Mormon laundry basket as the caption casually notes: "Some of the Washing Has to be Done Out" (see Fig. 82).[62] Still another cartoon used as its caption words attributed to the celebrated preacher De Witt Talmage: "The Chinese May Stay, but the Mormons Must Go" (Fig. 74).[63]

Harper's Weekly made the most of the comic "Mormon Bill" to convey another anti-Chinese opinion:

Mormon Bill, a resident of Utah, felt so deeply wounded by the President's veto of the anti-Chinese bill, that he loaned his new fourteen-dollar boots to complete the make-up of an effigy of General Arthur. While Bill was at his breakfast, some gamins set fire to the

---

53. Also appearing frequently in prints containing Chinese and Mormons was another familiar westerner, the native American.

54. *The Wasp*, 8 February 1879, p. 441.

55. Ibid., 23 August 1879, pp. 72–73.

56. Ibid., 2 April 1881, pp. 216–17.

57. Ibid., 16 December 1881, p. 385.

58. Ibid., 13 January 1882, pp. 24–25.

59. Ibid., 24 March 1882, p. 192.

60. Ibid., 5 June 1886, p. 16.

61. Ibid., 11 June 1887, pp. 8–9.

62. *The Judge*, 17 December 1881, pp. 8–9.

63. Ibid., 27 October 1883, p. 16.

stuffed figure, and barefooted Mormon Bill is now more hostile to the Chinese than ever before.[64]

Projecting the editorial view through a Mormon fall guy perpetuated the notion of Chinese as even more alien and threatening to American values than the laughable Mormons. Having Bill naively loan "his new fourteen-dollar boots" to an effigy of President Arthur subtly set Utahns over against the government and confirmed the stereotype of the intellectually backward Mormon. Such episodes amounted to a net loss in public image for both Mormons and Chinese.

The Mormon and Chinese questions were tied together in one other way. Why, asked *The Argonaut*, not apply the exclusionary legislation designed explicitly against the Chinese to prospective Mormon immigrants? But even though *The Argonaut* advocated restrictive immigration aimed at Mormons, its official editorial policy clearly reserved its most intense prejudices for Catholics and Chinese. While classifying Mormonism as "humbug" and an "excuse for breaking the law," the editors recognized some good qualities.

> The analogies between Mormons and Chinese do not hold good in any single particular. Mormons are not of distinctive race; they can and do assimilate with us; they come from branches of the human family to which we belong; they bring with them their wives and children, come to stay, acquire lands, and in all respects, save their religious belief—and that only as to the plurality of wives—do they pretty substantially agree with us in religious belief, and in many respects they are the best immigrants that come to the country, and except in this one peculiarity, they are good citizens. . .[65]

Such ambivalence may help explain why the exclusion of Mormon immigrants never became a legal reality. But most stereotyping and linking of unpopular minorities required single, unilinear condemnation.

Mormons and Native Americans

The idea of a formal alliance between Mormons and the Irish, Catholics, blacks, or Chinese was entirely imaginary. For Mormons and native Americans, however, the association was not as farfetched. After all, Mormon theology did express a special affinity and interest in the early inhabitants of the land including the notions of a cooperative, common destiny; they lived together as neighbors, though not always in a neighborly fashion, and held common grievances concerning their treatment by the United States government.[66] Brigham Young's

---

64. *Harper's Weekly*, 6 May 1882, p. 279.

65. *The Argonaut*, 17 October 1885, pp. 1–2.

66. On the long history of relations between Mormons and Indians, including the charges of collaboration, which began as early as the 1830s, see Leonard J. Arrington and Davis Bitton, *The Mormon Experience* (New York: Knopf, 1979), ch. 8, with accompanying notes.

policy "to feed them [rather] than to fight them" led many Indians to differentiate between Mormons and other Americans. This distinction fed suspicions of an unholy alliance. And when some Mormons in southern Utah, contrary to the expressed wishes of Brigham Young, enlisted the support of native Americans in the Mountain Meadows Massacre, the national image of Mormon-Indian complicity was reinforced. The connection took more than a half century to fade into oblivion.[67]

The vast majority of Mormon–American Indian prints played on emotions by rehashing the Mountain Meadows episode.[68] Others, noted earlier, simply depicted Mormons and Indians as common irritations to Uncle Sam. Still others generalized the sentiment of alleged Mormon-native American collusion. One illustration from this latter category appeared in *Yankee Notions* and showed the "Defiant Attitude of Brigham Young and Ye Indians Toward Ye Uncle Sam."[69] President Buchanan's dispatch of federal troops to Utah inspired the cartoon. Grotesque "savages" follow a heavily armed, bellicose Brigham Young attacking a United States gunboat presumably in the Great Salt Lake. The unruffled United States naval officer, a symbol of national confidence, peers through a telescope with equanimity at the advancing enemy. This idea of Brigham Young maneuvering native American recurred again and again.

Another drawing on this theme, executed by Thomas Nast for *Harper's Weekly*, was published fifty years after the earliest allegations of underhanded cooperation betwen the two minorities (Fig. 75).[70] Appearing on 18 February 1882, it gave additional thrust to the movement lobbying for enactment of the pending Edmunds anti-polygamy bill. Nast's thin "polygamous barbarian" promises "Much Guns, Much Ammunition, Much Whiskey" to an inebriated American Indian in exchange for "Much Kill Pale-Face." Powerful images are found in the subtle details: the blood of American soldiers dripping from the hands of the native American, the bodies of victims strewn about in the foreground and background, the Mormon Tabernacle looming suggestively in the distance. Weaving together

Fig. 75. "When Spring-time Comes, Gentle—Indian! *Polygamous Barbarian.* 'Much Guns, Much Ammunition, Much Whiskey, and Much Kill Pale-Face.' " From *Harper's Weekly*, 18 February 1882, drawn by Thomas Nast.

67. Juanita Brooks, *The Mountain Meadows Massacre* (Norman: University of Oklahoma Press, 1950).

68. Countless prints, including many reproductions, tapped this rich vein of emotion, suggestively inferring that the tragedy somehow typified what one might expect from Mormons. It was an unfair appraisal giving no attention to the complexity of events leading up to the encounter and oversimplifying motivation in the interest of propaganda.

69. *Yankee Notions*, April 1858, p. 111.

70. *Harper's Weekly,* 18 February 1882, p. 109. Nast's cartoon did not appear out of the blue. It was the result of reports of a Mormon–Indian alliance. Though Secretary Kirkwood "instructed the United States Indian agents to exercise the utmost diligence to ascertain the exact truth of these charges," Nast cut through the red tape of data collection to draw his own conclusions in the cartoon.

emotionally pregnant stereotypes to arouse the public was Nast's forte.

The penchant for pigeonholing certain groups in prints or printed material was symptomatic of a national malaise. Carried to its logical conclusion, it countenanced the denial of humanity and individuality as evidenced by such extreme measures as slavery, removal, persecution, and exclusion or the more ordinary condescension and derision. To justify sanctions society flagellated one group with the reputation of another. Deliberately manipulating and blending the imagery of unpopular minorities helped secure the social support for discrimination or oppression. The burden accompanying the identity of being a member of a particular minority was heavy enough. Sharing the collective weight of so-called negative traits of Mormons, Catholics, Irish, blacks, and native Americans was more than any single group ought to have borne. But such was the lot of "troublesome bedfellows."

5. Henry Ward Beecher And the Mormons

On a fitting day for fireworks, 4 July 1870, Lib Tilton confessed to her distinguished husband, Theodore, that she had been having an affair with the eminent minister Henry Ward Beecher. Partly out of deference for the woman he loved, the restrained Mr. Tilton kept any pyrotechnic display of emotion bottled up inside, with an occasional leak to a trusted confidant. And the troubled Lib, anxious to preserve the reputation of Beecher while renewing the affection of her husband, also found it impossible to conceal her secret. Eventually muted whisperings made their way to the national press. After a church investigation, a sensational trial by jury in 1875 aroused interest throughout the country. Beecher supporters interpreted the outcome—a hung jury—as an acquittal, but despite their protestations a cloud of suspicion followed the Reverend Beecher to his grave.[1]

Much to Beecher's dismay, the national press kept the controversy alive. Illustrations, puns, comic verse, and satirical articles with Beecher themes appeared in the humorous weeklies. "All the papers, from Brooklyn to the smallest hamlet in Oregon, are talking about it," said Charles A. Dana, "and the whole American people are anxious to know the truth."[2] Although Beecher's loyal followers still considered him an important element in the conscience of the nation, others viewed him as a symbol of religious hypocrisy. Other nationally known ministers, like De Witt Talmage were also subjected to journalistic ridicule. But so famous was Beecher as a man of the cloth and so flagrant was the moral turpitude that besmirched his name that this became a *cause célèbre* attracting attention for several years.[3]

Separated by hundreds of miles from Beecher's Brooklyn base, the Mormons would seem to have no possible connection with the scandal. Yet when Mormon leader Brigham Young died on 29 August 1877, the editors of *Puck* recognized a golden opportunity to thrust Mormons onto the Beecher battleground. This they did by a tongue-in-cheek nomination of Henry Ward Beecher as the successor to Brigham Young. The Mormons had already acquired the reputation, because of their polygamy, of being lecherous. Beecher had now the same reputation. Why

---

1. For two contrasting accounts of the Beecher-Tilton affair see: Paxton Hibben, *Henry Ward Beecher: An American Portrait* (New York: The Press of the Reader Club, 1942) and Lyman Abbot, *Henry Ward Beecher* (Boston: Houghton, Mifflin and Company, 1903).

2. Hibben, *Henry Ward Beecher*, p. 275.

3. Frank L. Mott, *A History of American Magazines, 1865–1885*, 5 vols. (Cambridge, Mass.: Harvard University Press, 1957), 3:87.

Fig. 76. "True Inwardness for Utah. H. W. B. sees by the *Herald* that Brigham Young leaves no successor, and promptly strikes for Salt Lake City, leaving Brooklyn disconsolate." Drawn by J. Keppler for *Puck*, 5 September 1877.

not kill two birds with one stone? Both Beecher and the Mormons could be ridiculed while entertaining the public.[4]

Using this connection, Keppler on the front cover of *Puck* on 5 September 1877 showed Beecher hurriedly departing by train for Salt Lake City, leaving another train of clinging, heartbroken damsels from Plymouth Congregational Church behind (Fig. 76).[5] An accompanying article entitled "Exit Brigham Young" drew the obvious conclusion: Henry Ward Beecher was "a man qualified by nature to lead the muchly married community." The writer went on to set forth the minister's qualifications as successor.

> He is younger than the dead prophet; he has the *suaviter in modo*, while not wanting in the *fortiter in re*.[6] There is no doubt in our minds that he will be enthusiastically welcomed by all the Mesdames Youngs, and the Young and old Youngs, and the sorrow of the afflicted wives, who at present refuse to be comforted, will be turned into unmixed joy when the news reaches them that Mr. Beecher has resolved to be a second husband to them, although we fear that certain circles in Brooklyn will suffer by his departure for fresh woods and pastures new.[7]

This same issue panned the Mormons by irreverently memorializing Brigham Young's death with the famous illustration of the vacated multiple marriage bed (Fig. 37).[8]

The proposal that Beecher succeed Brigham Young as head of the Mormons was so outlandishly humorous that *Puck's* editors thought it deserved repeating. The next several issues of the magazine featured variations of the theme. On 12 September *Puck* reported "wild enthusiasm" for Beecher's leadership of the Mormons as reflected in the flood of letters to the office of the humorous weekly "from all parts of the country." While this enthusiasm was overstated for effect, it is probable enough that the proposal met with humorous applause from the magazine's readers. The same issue contained a lighthearted fictitious inter-

---

4. The Mormons were not the only ones linked invidiously with Henry Ward Beecher. Grover Cleveland and Beecher were shown "painting the town red" in a full-page color cartoon. See *The Wasp* 27 September 1884, p. 1.

5. The title of the cartoon "True Inwardness for Utah" was a satirical allusion to the words "true inwardness" appearing in a letter from Beecher to Lib Tilton. "Should God inspire you to restore and rebuild at home, and while doing it to cheer and sustain outside of it another who sorely needs your help in heart and spirit, it will prove a life so noble as few are able to live. . . . If it would be a comfort to you, now and then, to send me a letter of *true inwardness* (our italics)—the outcome of your inner life— it would be safe, for I am now at home here with my sister, and it is permitted to you." Hibben, *Henry Ward Beecher*, pp. 231–32.

6. The English equivalent for the Latin *suaviter in modo, fortiter in re* is: Gentle in manner, resolute in execution.

7. *Puck*, 5 September 1877, p. 2.

8. This lithograph was so popular that separately printed copies sold out rapidly.

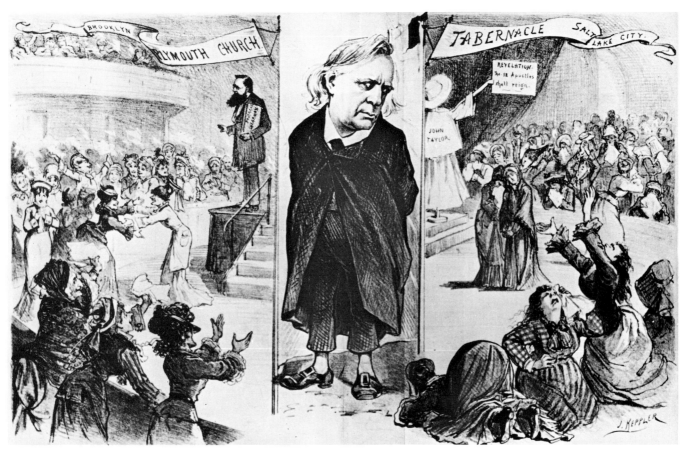

Fig. 77. "The Defeated Saint." *Puck*, 19 September 1877, drawn by J. Keppler.

view with "The Coming Mormon Prophet."[9] An aura of sensuality was created by describing Beecher's companion during the interview as a young, "pink-stockinged" beauty with "strawberry colored hair." Here is a sample of the suggestive dialogue:

Reporter: What do you think of Mormonism?
Beecher: As a religion it is heathenish, but as a social condition it has its advantages. It teaches the value of one good sound man weighed in the scale with many weak women.
Reporter: You bet on the good sound man every time, don't you?
Beecher: I do.

After hearing the preacher's reluctance to become an instant father of fifty-six children, the reporter "tried to reconcile Mr. Beecher to that feature of his office by painting delight in other quarters, and then left him looking very cheerful."

The following week, 19 September 1877, a double-page Keppler cartoon showed the women of Plymouth Church ecstatic, Mormon women beside themselves with disappoint-

9. *Puck*, 12 September 1877, p. 3.

THE DEAD PROPHET

One more polygamous
   Short in the breath,
Frightfully bigamous
   Gone to his death.

Turn not away from him,
   Scorning to touch;
Go nearer and pray for him
   Married so much.

Think of his fathers-in-law,
Two hundred brothers-in-law,
Three hundred sisters-in-law,
Fifty odd mothers-in-law,
   All in one family
   Left polygamily;

Think of their daily life,
Full of domestic strife,
   Cat-fights and squealings;
Think of the tears and cries,
Then try to Ann Elize[12]
   Some of their feelings.
Think of the weekly dues
And of the baby shoes
   And stockings unnumbered;
Think of the payments large,
Think of a daily charge
   Of an infant Six Hundred.

Oh! turn not away from him,
   Scorning to touch;
Go nearer and pray for him,
   Married so much.

Oh! this is pitiful!
With a city widows full,
   Buxom and fair.
Old bachelors, think of it;
Go near to the brink of it
   Now, if you dare.

Still for his bigamy
And muddy polygamy
   Leave him at rest:
Cross his hands humbly
As if praying dumbly,
   Over his breast;
Owing his weakness,
   The poor erring creature,
And leaving with meekness
   His mantle to Beecher.

ment, and Beecher "defeated," as the Mormon apostles had decided to collectively preside over the Mormon faith (Fig. 77). The main thrust of the cartoon was maligning the character of Henry Ward Beecher, but in the process Mormonism and women were neatly handled by uncomplimentary popular stereotypes. Tongue in cheek, the text editorialized:

> We are sorry for Henry, and so is a large majority of the Mormon people. He looks with wistful eyes towards the spot which he had fondly hoped would be the scene of his ministrations, where so much could be achieved . . .

> But Mr. Beecher is fervently loved by his flock, and their joy is unbounded especially among those of his admirers who are of the female persuasion.[10]

By the final week of September, James Penuckle published "The Dead Prophet" in the *Syracuse Herald*, and *Puck* reprinted the rhyme. Its meter was roughly that of Kipling's "The Charge of the Light Brigade"; the work was subtitled "A New Bridge of Sighs":[11]

Out on the West Coast, *The Wasp* wasted no time in picking up on the Beecher–Brigham Young theme.[13] Although the 22 September cover cartoon of women running from Mr. Beecher did not refer to Mormons, the accompanying article did. It began with a reference to Beecher's anticipated visit as the "awful calamity about to befall San Francisco." The satire proceeded in the same light vein. "We have had Dr. Mary Walker, Tilton, Ingersoll, Morton, Soldene, Eli Perkins,[14] a dry year and many other calamities during the year and survived them; but now Beecher is coming we must prepare for the worst. . . . Unless providence should interfere and mercifully change Beecher's mind, the time is not far distant when an earthquake will be welcomed as a pleasing change from the monotony of our afflictions." If Beecher were to visit Salt Lake City on his way and assume the leadership of the Mormons, the article continued, San Francisco might be spared the calamity. Such was the "only hope" of the author of the article. Who but Mormon women could deflect Beecher's interest from completing his trek farther West?

Faced with the ominous prospect of a pending visit, the article

10. Ibid., 19 September 1877, p. 2.

11. Ibid., 26 September 1877, p. 13.

12. Ann Elize was a play on words referring to Ann Eliza Young, the disenchanted wife of Brigham Young who left him and the Mormon church and lectured and wrote about her experiences among the Mormons. See Chapter 2, note 32.

13. *The Wasp*, 22 September 1877, p. 115.

14. Dr. Mary Walker was a well-known feminist and physician. Ingersoll was an outspoken agnostic. Morton was a prominent politician. Soldene was an actress of note, and Eli Perkins was the pen name for a popular humorist. All were numbered among the calamities cited in the article.

continued in a mock-serious vein. Poets were summoned "to manufacture a dirge for the occasion, and, after much wrestling with the unwilling muse, the following was evolved:

> A mighty man is coming here
>   A most distinguished preacher,
> Whose name is known both far and near,
>   We mean H. W. Beecher.
>
> He comes upon the "ragged edge"[15]
>   With love on every feature
> O! Parents with your handsome girls,
>   Look out for Parson Beecher!
>
> Don't let your wife go running round
>   But earnestly beseech her
> To stay at home and mind the house,
>   And never look at Beecher.
>
> "True Inwardness"[16] is in his soul
>   This pious Plymouth teacher
> He's now the boss since Brigham died,
>   So much for Mr. Beecher.

One friend of the Mormons, the erratic George Francis Train, thought the comparison between Beecher and Young unfair to the Mormon leader. In a lengthy versified obituary of Brigham Young, Train wrote:[17]

> The difference 'twixt Brigham and Beecher,
> The Mormon prophet and the Christian preacher,
> Was, Brigham Young to his wives was true,
> While Beecher on other households grew!
> One turned Polygamy to Monogamy,
> The other, Monogamy to Polygamy!
> Beecher, one wife, with others free,
> Brigham, many, but no adultery!

Such broad-minded approval of polygamy, while often found in the statements of Mormon defenders, was seldom agreed to by outside observers.

As the Mormons closed ranks behind new leadership, humorists had to discover other ways of relating Beecher to the Mormons. In the spring of 1878 Joseph Keppler brought Beecher and Mormonism together again at an international exhibit held in Paris (Fig. 78). Keppler designed "A Truly Representative American Exhibit"[18] for a *Puck* cartoon which consisted of an

---

15. "Ragged-edge" was the name given to a letter written by H. W. Beecher to a friend, Frank Moulton. "But to live on the sharp and ragged edge of anxiety, remorse, fear, despair, and yet to put on all the appearance of serenity and happiness, cannot be endured much longer." Hibben, *Henry Ward Beecher*, p. 238.

16. See note 6, above.

17. "The Death of Brigham Young," *Deseret Evening News*, 17 October 1877.

18. *Puck*, 15 May 1878, pp. 8–9.

Fig. 78. "A Truly Representative American Exhibit Arranged by Puck for the Paris Exhibition." *Puck*, 15 May 1878, drawn by J. Keppler.

agrarian showcase of inferior American products—personalities, ethnic and religious groups, and unpopular causes and conditions. The alcoholic Irishman appears on a label entitled "Micks on Irish Whiskey"; blacks are caricatured in a bottle of "Black-Berry Jam." Associated groups pictured include "Pickeled Tramps," "White Trash," "Spiritualist," and "Dried Hoodlums," among others. Front and center in the cartoon, a dubious distinction, were two large plants labeled "Mormonism" and "Beecherism." The flowers growing out of "Beecherism" fittingly formed a triangle of faces with Beecher and Theodore Tilton looking competitively toward the indecisive Lib Tilton. Similarly, the more fruitful plant of Mormonism showed eleven flowering female beauties surrounding a contented John Taylor, the Mormon leader. The similarity of caricature and proximity of the two plants was not coincidental.

In the fall of 1878, the Beecher–Mormonism association was kept alive in *Puck* from material borrowed out of the *Philadelphia Kronicle–Herald.* "The Mormon women of Salt Lake City have resolved that polygamy is a divine institution and conducive to long life and strength. Perhaps this explains why Beecher keeps so remarkably healthy."[19]

19. Ibid., 27 November 1878, p. 13.

Fig. 79. "The Religious Vanity Fair." *Puck*, 22 October 1879, drawn by J. Keppler.

On 22 October 1879, Beecher and Mormonism appeared jointly in one more *Puck* cartoon (Fig. 79). The intent of this illustration was to poke fun at the particularistic, only-road-to-salvation claims of diverse religions. Spiritualists, Catholics, Baptists, Methodists, Presbyterians, Episcopalians, Seventh-Day Adventists, and Jews were all humorously caricatured with popular stereotypes befitting each faith.[20] Predictably, the caricatures of Henry Ward Beecher and the Mormons were strikingly similar. Beecher was shown on a couch with a beckoning finger. Two insinuating signs suggestive of lasciviousness—"White Souls for Sale" and "Beecher's only 'Love' Road to Heaven, Sleeping Car Attached"—hung over the Beecher booth. A nest, which had ribald connotations for those who had followed the Beecher scandal, was also part of the scene.[21] Similarly, a bearded,

20. The point of the *Puck* cartoon was that organized religions had missed the boat in their claims to showing the way of salvation. In the hands of the cupid-like Puck in the corner of the cartoon was the obvious answer penned on a sign: "The Best Route [to salvation]—Clean Hands and a Pure Heart." *Puck*, 22 October 1879, pp. 526–27.

21. Once again the nest symbol, like "true inwardness" and "ragged-edge," came from Beecher correspondence of some kind. Lib Tilton wrote to Beecher: ". . . in all the sad complications of the past years, my endeavor was entirely to keep from you all suffering, to bear myself alone, leaving you forever ignorant of it. My weapons were love, a larger untiring generosity

old, leering Mormon, with young women on each arm and a canopied bed in the background, stood under a sign reminiscent of the Beecher slur. It read: "Polygamy—The Only Sure and Pleasant Road of Salvation." These visual associations were certain to perpetuate the mental connection which many had learned concerning Beecher and Mormonism. The Mormons were for Beecher what the unpopular "Turks" had been for the Mormons—a pictorial signal of lasciviousness.[22]

So from coast to coast humorists had fun at the expense of Beecher and the "peculiar" inhabitants of Utah. But what did Beecher really think of the Mormons? Did he clearly disassociate himself from them? Why not attack them, even recommend their extermination, as his ministerial colleague, the Reverend De Witt Talmage, did? Didn't he have everything to gain and nothing to lose by joining the chorus of criticism?

To be sure, Beecher declared himself unequivocally against polygamy. Not all of the opponents of polygamy were happy about Beecher's identification with their cause. "The Rev. Henry Ward Beecher is a bitter and uncompromising enemy of polygamy," wrote the *Grand Rapids Times*. "If those wicked Mormons get hold of this information they'll be sure to use it as a campaign document; and it isn't a bad argument on their side of the question either." The *Deseret Evening News* did indeed get hold of the information and took advantage of Beecher's apparent hypocrisy. "We are always gratified to learn of the opposition of persons like the unsavory leader of the new Brooklyn revival. We never knew a lecherous man or woman yet who was not an 'uncompromising enemy' of 'Mormon' plural marriage."[23]

However, Beecher did not see the Mormons as an unmitigated evil. The most comprehensive exposition of his ambivalent opinions about the Mormons was contained in a lengthy Thanksgiving Day address delivered at Plymouth Church in 1883.[24] Beecher had just recently visited Salt Lake City, lectured

---

and nest-hiding! . . ." Hibben, *Henry Ward Beecher*, p. 231. An interesting rhyme appeared in a California periodical with reference to the new vocabulary generated by the Beecher scandal:

> "Beecher your words survive their parents acts—
> 'Nest hiding,' 'ragged edge,' and 'bottom facts'
> Prove how you prospered in your noble aim
> To vulgarize the lexicon of shame."
> *The Argonaut*, 25 January 1879, p. 9.

22. To fix an unfavorable image of Mormonism, Mormons were often pictured in Turkish dress or described as "Turks" to associate them with a foreign brand of polygamy.

23. For both the *Grand Rapids Times* and *Deseret Evening News* statements see Journal History, 16 March 1881. The Journal History is a large, multivolume compilation of material, mainly from newspapers, located in the Historical Department of the Church of Jesus Christ of Latter-day Saints, Salt Lake City, Utah.

24. *Deseret Evening News*, 6 December 1883.

in the Salt Lake Theatre, and been taken on a personal tour of the city by the leader of the Mormons, John Taylor. His parishioners were anxious to hear about his visit. He titillated them by noting that many of the Mormon leaders were present at his lecture in Salt Lake City "and so many of their wives as could be spared (laughter)." He deplored the "ignoble origin" of Mormonism, but conceded it was "one of the great forces of modern society." Consistent with the prevailing nativist spirit in America, he identified the bulk of Mormon immigrants as poor and ignorant, but went on to acknowledge that the majority "rise at once and by their industry and frugality become at once better men and acquire property." He found it "odious . . . to have such a stink pot right in the midst of the nation." Yet there was some admiration for the Mormons' commitment to their religion: "If our people here believed half so much in Christianity as the people of Utah did in Mormonism, we would see the globe revolutionized."

One of the qualities Beecher noted in Mormondom was orderliness. "No more orderly city exists on this continent than Salt Lake City," he wrote. But this quality Beecher attributed to an "absolute spiritual despotism," which he explained as a curious government by irrigation. "The Mormon lives on a farm that is irrigated by water which the church owns and controls. The church has only to stop the water from his farm and the sinful or objectionable Mormon will starve or repent. No court, no trial, no anything—simply shut the gates. I think there never was so efficient a government so simply executed in the world (laughter)."

Even on polygamy, which Beecher opposed, he uttered some words that were not displeasing to the Mormons. This was in a lecture delivered in 1885:

> But if the Bible is the word of God according to the old theory of plenary direct inspiration, then Mormonism is right—this is its stronghold today. They believe in the Old Testament—they believe in it like thunder! When any man should undertake to hold at one and the same time the absolute inspiration, according to the old verbal theory of the Bible, how is he going to get away from that declaration, "Mormonism canot be wrong, for God inspired it, and you have got it in His book."

Certainly Beecher was attempting to buttress his rejection of plenary verbal inspiration of the scriptures by showing that acceptance of such a premise would lead to an unacceptable conclusion. But Mormons were quick to agree that Mormonism was "the religion of the Bible if there is any Bible religion on the earth. . . ."[25]

---

25. *Ogden Herald*, 16 June 1885. Cf. the slightly different wording in Henry W. Beecher, *Evolution and Religion* (New York: Fords, Howard & Hulbert, 1885), p. 66.

He proposed a solution to the "Mormon problem" in the 1883 Thanksgiving sermon. After explaining how much he disliked the Mormon system, he quickly made a distinction: he hated the institution but he loved the Mormons. In the final analysis, he said, there were only two ways of dealing with them. Beecher rejected the first solution—putting them to the sword (some were seriously advocating the use of military force). He favored the second solution—to "let them alone," which actually meant to him using moral influence, preaching, and education.

A survey of reactions to Henry Ward Beecher in the Mormon press reveals as much ambivalence by the Mormons toward Beecher as he had exhibited toward the Mormons. The celebrated preacher's lectures received mixed reviews from the Mormons. When he lectured on "The Wasted and Burdens of Society" in Salt Lake City in 1878, the *Deseret News* said:

> Opinions as to the merits and demerits of the lecture, are as various as opinions generally are, some pronouncing it to be a crowning gem of oratory, others, equally vehement, berating it as a fraud upon the public. These are the extremes, however, equally unreliable. It is safe to say that the large majority of those who heard it were highly entertained by the ventilation of the subject, which, though by no means new, was presented in a very pleasant and attractive manner, while their curiosity, at the same time, was gratified at beholding the noted personage whose name Madame Rumor for a number of years, has handled so freely and unmercifully.[26]

Attempting to strike a middle ground and mentioning the scandal only briefly seemed to be a rather sensible reaction.

In 1883 Beecher spoke again in the Salt Lake Theatre, this time on "The Moral Uses of Riches, Luxury and Beauty." For the church newspaper the lecture provided ample evidence that Beecher's "staple patrons are the rich and affluent, whose ears could not fail to be tickled with the general tenor of his theory." His platform manner was evaluated as follows:

> Two or three times his memory appeared to fail him, but with the adroitness of the experienced orator he covered up this fact from the bulk of the audience by pleasantly uttering common placeisms until he was enabled to again seize the thread of his story. He is a most attractive speaker, maintaining the ordinary, conversational tone through the bulk of his lecture, causing the more pathetic and emphatic passages to stand out with all the more striking conspicuosity when he threw into them the full force of his energetic and passionate nature.[27]

As in the earlier reaction the Mormons were appreciative but had not lost their sense of distance or their critical faculty.

When Beecher made remarks about the Mormons, their reaction was predictable: favorable if his comments had been

---

26. *Deseret Evening News*, 12 September 1878.
27. Ibid., 12 September 1883.

positive, critical if he had denounced them or if, from their point of view, he had been inaccurate. The 1883 Thanksgiving sermon was printed in its entirety—at least the section discussing the Mormons—in Salt Lake City. Appreciative of his praise and gratified by his "leave them alone" recommendation, they nevertheless felt free to take issue at certain points.[28] They did not like his assumption that the New Testament could be used to refute the Old Testament practices of the Mormons. "Christ came not to 'whip out' or destroy Moses and the prophets, but to fulfill their sayings, and Mormonism cannot be assailed by the teachings of Jesus and the Apostles," said the *Deseret News*. His humorous claim that Mormons were kept under control by threats to cut off their water was flatly denied: "Every possessor of water rights is protected therein by that [secular] law, and the idea that he can be summarily deprived of them in the way described by Mr. Beecher is entirely incorrect."

By contrast with the militant demands of some anti-Mormon critics, however, Henry Ward Beecher seemed mild indeed. The Mormons praised his humanity, his common sense, his fairness. One woman wrote of her longstanding admiration for his writings.[29] She had given him the benefit of the doubt when hearing of the scandal and praised his "stamina of mind and spirit" exhibited at the trial; an inferior character, she thought, "would have taken repose in suicide." She deplored any implied aspersions on the character of Mormon women but thought that much in his Thanksgiving address "had the right ring in it, even the aroma of truth and justice."

When Beecher died, in 1887, there was a complimentary editorial in the *Deseret Evening News*.[30] Later a belated defense of his innocence in the Beecher-Tilton scandal appeared.[31] Perhaps the ultimate compliment from the Mormons, however, was an editorial acknowledgment that Beecher may have received divine inspiration: "But why should not a Beecher at times have been

---

28. For disagreements with some of Beecher's doctrinal ideas, see *The Journal of Discourses* 26 vols. (Liverpool, Engl.: Albert Carrington, 1854–86), 24:74; 26:219, 307, sermons delivered 6 April 1883, 31 May 1885, and 28 August 1885 respectively. For an editorial challenge of his views on a future life, see *Deseret News Weekly*, 28 September 1877.

29. *Deseret Evening News*, 9 December 1883.

30. Journal History, 8 March 1887.

31. "New Particulars seem to have come to light in the once famous Henry Ward Beecher trial, by which the noted preacher is cleared of every lingering shadow of suspicion. . . . Henry Ward Beecher ranked high among the Protestant preachers of this century. He was a power in our national life. It is therefore gratifying to the American public to learn that every stain on his memory has been removed. His friends, of course, never doubted his innocence, but a spot on a clerical robe is difficult to remove. It is much better to know that it never existed except in the imagination of the uninformed or the fabrications of enemies." Journal History, 28 August 1900.

under special divine influence?"[32] It was a fitting conclusion to a relationship which began with guilt by association and ended with a mutual, if ambivalent and cautious, admiration.

32. Journal History, 9 February 1904.

From the Colonial period through the golden era of political cartoons by Thomas Nast and Joseph Keppler to the present, political fortune has often been linked to the art of caricature. "Boss" Tweed, Andrew Jackson, Susan B. Anthony, Abraham

6. Political Caricature And Mormonism

Fig. 80. "Puck to Columbia: These are the Old Year Legacies to the New—A pretty Lot of Work for '82." Drawn by J. Keppler for *Puck*, 28 December 1881.

Lincoln, and Theodore Roosevelt are only a few of the personalities cartoonists satirized. Issues such as woman's suffrage, slavery, populism, free silver, and monopolies were frequently illustrated.[1] Mormonism also entered into this cauldron of causes and characters; however, in histories of political caricature there is only token recognition given to Mormon subjects and to the illustrators and cartoonists who used Mormon themes.[2]

Few political issues matched the durability of the clash of values between American society and the Mormons. The history of the Mormon graphic image explored in earlier chapters dem-

1. Allen Nevins and Frank Weitenkampf, *A Century of Political Cartoons* (New York: Charles Scribner's Sons, 1944), p. 16.

2. Ibid.; Stephen Hess and Milton Kaplan, *The Ungentlemanly Art: A History of American Political Cartoons* (New York: Macmillan Co., 1968); Thomas C. Blaisdell, Jr., and Peter Selz, *The American Presidency in Political Cartoons, 1776–1976* (Salt Lake City: Peregrine Smith, Inc., 1976).

Fig. 81. "The Same Thing Over Again." Drawn by James A. Wales for *The Judge*, 17 December 1881.

Fig. 82. "The Too Much Married; Or Mormon Domestic Bliss." Thomas Worth drew this for *The Judge*, 17 December 1881.

onstrates that the Utah War, presidential edicts, anti-polygamy legislation, Supreme Court decisions, the refusal to seat Congressmen from Utah, and the grudging acceptance of a Mormon United States senator were subjects often featured by illustrators. And many of the hundreds of illustrations featuring Mormons showed them entangled in national political issues.

The Mormon Image as a Weapon

Astute caricaturists like Louis Maurer, Thomas Worth, Bernard and Victor Gillam, Phillip G. Cusachs, James A. Wales, and others presented Mormons in two political contexts. One set of illustrations appealed to the executive and legislative branches of government to eliminate the practice of polygamy. Another collection of prints manipulated the Mormon image in conjunction with presidential political campaigns. Some cartoonists exploited the Mormon question to defame political opponents. Others blew the trumpet of their candidate's ability to solve the Mormon issue. From James Buchanan through Teddy Roosevelt, a half century of political activity, Mormonism was a frequent theme for political caricaturists.

In 1856 the Republicans denounced "the twin relics of barbarism" and added an anti-polygamy plank to the anti-slavery provision in their platform.[3] In a Currier and Ives campaign print, the Republican presidential standard bearer, John C. Frémont, is shown gaining momentum over a beleaguered Buchanan, who cries, "Oh dear! Oh dear! This platform will be the death of me. I'm nearly crushed out already" (Fig. 83). In the background on the top of the Rocky Mountains flies an American flag, suggesting that if the Republicans prevailed, Americanism not Mormonism would be firmly planted in that area. This modest beginning marked the introduction of Mormon themes in political cartooning.

Buchanan won the election, of course, and ironically it was he, not Frémont, who sent federal troops to Utah in 1857. Known historically as the "Utah War," this expedition turned out to be more of a skirmish than an actual military confrontation. But in the press words and cartoons battered Mormonism and gave it greater visibility.[4]

During the 1860 campaign for the presidency, supporters of Stephen A. Douglas thought they detected an Achilles heel in Lincoln's position on the Mormons. Louis Maurer, one of the more prolific illustrators for Currier and Ives, portrayed Mor-

3. The most probable candidates for earlier political cartoons on the Mormons are the 1844 and 1852 presidential elections. Joseph Smith ran for the presidency of the United States in 1844, but was martyred that same year. As noted in Chapter 1, we have searched in vain for cartoons including Joseph Smith as a presidential candidate; we haven't found anything from the presidential election of 1852 either.

4. See Gary L. Bunker and Davis Bitton, "Illustrated Periodical Images

Fig. 83. Currier and Ives lithograph, "The Balls Are Rolling—Clear the Track" (1856).

Fig. 84. "The Mormon Problem Solved. *Brigham*—'I must submit to your laws—but what shall I do with all these?' *U. S. G.*—'Do as I do—give them offices.'" *Leslie's Weekly*, 11 November 1871, drawn by Morgan.

monism, Free Love, Women's Rights, Socialism, and other controversial positions of the day as the backbone of the Lincoln candidacy (Fig. 16). "By the unanimous consent of the people" Horace Greeley carries Abe Lincoln into the "Lunatic Asylum," the "Right House" for Lincoln rather than the White House. Predictably, the Mormon in the cartoon stands next to the proponents of Free Love, arms linked together for maximum associative effect. In 1856 Maurer had used an almost identical cartoon to malign Frémont; now, in 1860, the symbol of Mormonism was substituted for that of Catholicism.[5] On the basis of such guilt by association one journalist asked the patently unfair question "Is Mr. Lincoln a Mormon?"[6]

When Mormonism again became an issue after the Civil War, in 1871 Matt Morgan of *Leslie's Weekly* took up where Louis Maurer left off (Fig. 84). In this cartoon Brigham Young says, "I must submit to your laws—but what shall I do with all these?"—referring to his huge family.[7] Ulysses S. Grant replies, "Do as I do—give them offices." The corruption of the Grant administration and the "Mormon problem" were thus ridiculed in the same cartoon.

After Grant's two terms, Rutherford B. Hayes urged Congress to enact more decisive anti-polygamy legislation. But the Congress seemed in no mood to act on the Utah question. However, other events were happening that would nudge a reluctant Congress. A Supreme Court decision overturning the conviction of the Utah polygamist Owen Miles aroused public opinion.[8]

of Mormons, 1850–1860," *Dialogue: A Journal of Mormon Thought* 10 (Spring 1977): 82–94.

5. Nevins and Weitenkampf, *A Century of Political Cartoons*, pp. 76–77.

6. *Deseret News*, 26 June 1857, reprinted from *Missouri Republican*.

7. *Leslie's Weekly*, 11 November 1871, p. 137.

8. The Supreme Court ruled that the lower court failed to produce evidence of a marriage.

Nearly three decades had elapsed since the official acknowledgment of polygamy. Artists for *The Judge, Puck, The Wasp, Harper's Weekly,* and *The Daily Graphic* displayed their disdain for the tortoise-like pace of government. To reach the most sensitive nerve, they concentrated on the Presidency. In *The Daily Graphic,* a Phillip G. Cusachs cartoon pictures Hayes leaving office in 1881 with a bag of unfulfilled intentions, among them a symbol of Mormonism.[9] Campaign promises bulging from under his arms, Garfield begins his ascent up the White House steps with the scroll "Extermination of Polygamy in Utah." Less than one month later James A. Garfield was cartooned as a gladiator unsheathing the sword of "National Authority" against the dragon of polygamy (Fig. 85).[10] Vultures hover above and the carcass of slavery rests under the other "twin relic." The caption reads: "Complete the work begun by the Republican party twenty years ago."

Out on the West Coast, Frederick Keller of *The Wasp* created a double-page color lithograph showing Garfield, axe in hand, ready to fell the tree of Mormonism.[11] Watchful faces of prominent Mormon personalities gaze from the tree. In the background two other trees are labeled slavery and "Chinese curse." Lincoln's name is inscribed on the axe lying next to the felled slavery tree and a question mark appears on the axe by the tree symbolizing anti-Chinese sentiment. Uncle Sam and the congressional axe sharpener round out the cartoon imagery. The message is clear. Lincoln has done his duty. Garfield will take care of Mormonism. Now who will step forward to deal with the Chinese?[12]

A Stormy Decade

When the hand of an assassin prematurely ended the life of James A. Garfield in 1881, some intemperate partisans tried to whip up sentiment against the Mormons during the period of national mourning. "I will not say that he [the assassin] was a Mormon," cried the Reverend T. De Witt Talmage, "but he has all the Mormon theories. . . . He had the ugliness of a Mormon, the licentiousness of a Mormon, the cruelty of a Mormon, the murderous spirit of a Mormon, the infernalism of a Mormon. . . . I should not wonder if, in the great day when all secret things are revealed, it should be found that he was a paid agent

Fig. 85. "Complete the Work Begun by the Republican Party Twenty Years Ago." *The Daily Graphic,* 23 February 1881.

9. *The Daily Graphic,* 28 January 1881, p. 651. Phillip G. Cusachs was director of art for the *Daily Graphic.* Frank Weitenkampf, *American Graphic Art* (New York: The Macmillan Co., 1924), p. 187.

10. *The Daily Graphic,* 23 February 1881, p. 853.

11. *The Wasp,* 2 April 1881, pp. 216–17.

12. Actually, though not reflected in the cartoon, *The Wasp* was rather ambivalent about the anti-Mormon crusade. Editorially, they lauded the achievements of their fellow Westerners and expressed genuine concern over what they considered violations of religious liberties. For example, see *The Wasp,* 14 August 1880, 26 March 1881, and 2 April 1881.

Fig. 86. "An Unsightly Object—Who Will Take the Axe and Hew It Down?" *The Judge*, 28 January 1882, drawn by Wales.

Fig. 87. "One Wife or No Ballot." *The Judge*, 4 March 1882.

of that old hag of hell."[13] A *Puck* cartoon showed Garfield bowing out of mortality, leaving Chester A. Arthur a legacy of unresolved problems, including the snake of Mormonism (Fig. 80).[14] This verbal and visual imagery encouraged enthusiasm for political action, and President Garfield's death added momentum to the forces lobbying for more stringent measures against polygamy.

Another illustrated weekly, *The Judge*, now mounted a relentless attack on Mormonism. A cover cartoon by James A. Wales declared *The Judge's* expectations for the new President (Fig. 81).[15] The caption, "The Same Thing Over Again," was a reminder that Ulysses S. Grant and Rutherford B. Hayes had uttered the same refrain, "The Mormons Must Go," without tangible results. In the same issue *The Judge* enlisted Thomas Worth's talent (Fig. 82).[16] He satirized "Mormon Domestic Bliss" by portraying avaricious wives going through the pockets of their husbands' pants, an oversized baby buggy, an enormous Mormon laundry basket, huge medicine containers for the Mormon family, a gigantic money pouch for tickets to the circus, Mormon wives greeting a delinquent husband with broomsticks, and the Mormon male favoring the younger over the older wife. The lithograph by itself appears more like social rather than political caricature, but the commentary directed "to the lawmakers of the nation" suggests explicit political intent.

> Look at that poor foolish man, surrounded by his furious wives, and ask yourselves whether he shall not be rescued from his misery! Glance at the horror of his situation, when taking his children to the wives, and let your tears flow fast! Think of his washing bills and all the rest, and call yourselves protectors of your fellow-men if you dare, if you do not move hand or foot in their behalf in Mormondom! In submitting these pictures to the national legislators, the Judge asks them, in the name of all that is worth living for, to rise in their might, and with their strong voices blast from this continent the foul blot of Mormonism upon it, so that it may never take shape again, permitting every American to shout, "one flag, one country, and one wife!"[17]

Just one month later another Wales cartoon appeared, this time more hostile, with the caption "An Unsightly Object, Who Will Take the Axe and Hew It Down?" (Fig. 86)[18] Senator Edmunds of Vermont stands in the background. Once again

13. T. De Witt Talmage, *Selected Sermons*, 20 vols. (New York: Louis Klopsch, 1900): 2:205–7. The humorist Bill Nye cast similar aspersions on the Mormons in *The Argonaut*, 8 October 1881, p. 2. The reaction of the Mormons to Garfield's death was one of genuine mourning and sympathy for the fallen president and his family. See *Deseret Evening News*, 20 September 1881.

14. *Puck*, 28 December 1881, pp. 268–69.

15. *The Judge*, 17 December 1881, p. 1.

16. Ibid., pp. 8–9.

17. Ibid., p. 2.

18. Ibid., 28 January 1882, pp. 8–9.

verbal commentary reinforces the graphic message: "Is there a man in Congress who has a moral and political record clean enough to come boldly out and attack this evil of Mormonism, and if there is such a one, has he got patriotism enough . . . to go thus to the front?"[19] *The Judge* concluded that no congressional champion had come forth "because he has not the brains to do so, or because they fear that their own moral record is not good enough and strong enough to enable them to grapple with moral reform of the Mormon dimensions." Meanwhile *Harper's Weekly*, *Leslie's Weekly*, *Puck*, and *The Wasp* were exerting their own graphic form of political pressure.[20]

Later Senator Edmunds came forth and President Arthur signed the Edmunds Act into law on 22 March 1882 denying Mormons practicing polygamy the right to vote or to hold public office.[21] *The Judge* celebrated with a cartoon entitled "One Wife or No Ballot" (Fig. 87).[22] The accompanying text editorialized: "The Judge observes with much satisfaction that the newspaper press of the country, State legislatures, popular orators, and distinguished clergymen have combined in an assault upon polygamy and although it is rather late in the day to begin the crusade against the defiant law-breakers of Utah, 'it is better late than never.'"[23]

Late in 1883, when it became clear that the Edmunds Act had not ended the practice of polygamy, *The Daily Graphic* featured about a dozen illustrations with such captions as: "What Does Congress Propose To Do About It?" "What Is Uncle Sam Going To Do About It?" "The Edmund's Law Is a Failure—What Shall Uncle Sam Do Next?"[24]

Many of *The Daily Graphic* illustrations were extreme (Figs. 88, 89, 90, 91, 92, 93, 94, 95, 96). One, featuring Mormon President John Taylor, proposed partitioning the Territory of Utah and giving sections to the adjoining territories of Nevada, Colorado, Wyoming, and Arizona.[25] Actually this was not a new proposal. In 1854 Benjamin Ferris reasoned:

> The Mormon power may be frittered away or neutralized by dividing the territory into parcels, and annexing them to New Mexico, Kansas, Nebraska and Oregon. This would leave them in a minority in each

19. Ibid., p. 2.

20. *Harper's Weekly*, 18 February 1882, p. 109; *Leslie's Weekly*, 4 February 1882, p. 409; *Puck* 25 January 1882; *The Wasp*, 24 March 1882, p. 192.

21. George Q. Cannon was denied his seat as the territorial representative to the Congress about the same time that the Edmund's legislation was passed.

22. *The Judge*, 4 March 1882, pp. 8–9.

23. Ibid., p. 2.

24. See *The Daily Graphic*, 21 August 1883; 22 October 1883; 1 November 1883.

25. *The Daily Graphic*, 9 March 1882, p. 57.

Fig. 88. "The Modern Bluebeard." *The Daily Graphic*, 21 August 1883.

Fig. 89. "The Remaining Twin." *The Daily Graphic*, 15 October 1883.

Fig. 90. "The Mormon Question." *The Daily Graphic*, 22 October 1883.

Fig. 91. "Shall Not That Sword Be Drawn?" *The Daily Graphic*, 25 October 1883.

Fig. 92. "What Shall They Do To Be Saved?" *The Daily Graphic*, 1 November 1883.

Fig. 93. "The Great Sin of the Century." *The Daily Graphic*, 12 December 1883.

of these territories; place the machinery of government beyond their control; and prevent them from making civil functions the instruments of ecclesiastical oppression.[26]

Another cartoon in *The Daily Graphic* indicated that plowing up Mormonism was "too mild"; something "more like an explosion" was needed.[27] Still another suggested extermination of Mormons as "The Only Sure Way."[28] C. S. Reinhart added to the visual stereotype of Mormonism by picturing a defiant, unscrupulous Mormon exclaiming, "We will fight God, Heaven and President Arthur before we give in."[29] President Arthur did not flinch at the challenge. His December 1883 message threatening to deprive Utah of any remaining semblance of self-government was depicted in a Phillip Cusachs cartoon on the cover of *The Daily Graphic*.[30]

One cartoonist said legislators from both parties ignored the Mormon problem because the issue could not "be used as a Presidential boom."[31] But used it was, and extensively so. For more than a quarter of a century, Democratic presidential candidates had gone to the political well and drawn up empty buckets. This year, with Grover Cleveland, the prospects looked better. To frustrate Cleveland's political aspirations, the Republicans prepared a campaign strategy which included portraying him as sympathetic to Mormonism. For several reasons Cleveland was vulnerable to this tactic. First, the Republicans had conceived, organized, and implemented anti-Mormon policies for nearly thirty years. They could claim success in opposing both polygamy and slavery. In contrast, the Democratic party had been, if not a proponent of slavery, at least an advocate of states' rights. It would be natural for the voter to surmise that as a states' rights advocate Cleveland might go easy on Mormonism. Second, the Mormons had not fared well under Republican leadership. Who could blame them for desiring change? Yet any suspicions of Mormon leanings toward Cleveland would hardly ingratiate him with other voters. Third, unfair whisperings of indiscreet moral behavior had created the Cleveland "scandal," which could easily be linked with the image of the stereotypic lustful Mormon. Finally, Cleveland's rotund contours and full-jowled face were readily identified with the similar cartoonist's version of the generalized Mormon, a portly imitation of Brigham Young.

As the presidential campaign between James G. Blaine and

26. Benjamin G. Ferris, *Utah and the Mormons* (New York: AMS Press, 1971), p. 369.
27. *The Daily Graphic*, 12 December 1883, p. 311.
28. Ibid., 6 December 1883, p. 267.
29. Ibid., 15 October 1883, p. 763.
30. Ibid., 4 December 1883, p. 251.
31. Ibid., 11 December 1883, p. 303.

Grover Cleveland drew to a close in 1884, *The Judge's* witty Thomas Worth used linguistic and artistic symbols to good advantage.[32] "Congenial Company," "The Mormons for Cleveland—Birds of a Feather Flock Together," and "The Cleveland Scandal" all delivered punches to the Cleveland midsection. "For Salt River," a symbol of defeat, tied in nicely with "From Salt Lake"—no symbol of distinction in those days (Fig. 97). Physiognomically similar, Cleveland links arms with the hefty Mormon. By any standard, this was effective political caricature.

A cartoon published in the short-lived *Jingo* deserves recognition as a significant example of American political caricature. Grover Cleveland and Mormonism were again the subjects (Fig. 98).[33] "We are with the Democratic party," says the Mormon Bishop Hart, "because its tendency is to restore individual rights." Bishop Hart is shown hanging a huge portrait of Grover Cleveland in the center of the room with small pictures of the Mormon leaders Joseph Smith and Brigham Young dramatizing the supposed Mormon adulation of Cleveland. Meanwhile, a young Mormon boy tramples with impunity on a portrait of George Washington. Additional negative images included a cluttered room, animals on the barren floor, cracks in the ceiling, and a revolver sticking out of the back pocket of the Mormon bishop. Although no additional comment was really necessary, a lengthy caption noted:

> This is really interesting. That all Utah was on fire with enthusiasm for Grover Cleveland, we had anticipated. In fact, that is one portion of the Union which might be expected to rise up with irresistible determination in his behalf. The principal difficulty is that Utah does not vote. But possibly its reason for favoring the Democratic party may impress themselves strongly upon the minds of citizens elsewhere. A restoration of "individual rights" to the Mormon husbands of twenty wives, and fathers of one hundred children each, really is a matter of great National concern. As to Governor Cleveland's opinions on that subject, the world is content to be left to inference.

Like blacks, Jews, native Americans, and the Irish of the period, Mormons were powerless to counteract such exaggerated imagery.

Other cartoons appeared in the same vein. *Jingo* linked Cleveland with Mormonism, Slavery, Scandal, Fraud, Repudiation, States' Rights, Secession, Tissue Ballots, Ku Klux Klan, Free Trade, and Bourbonism (Fig. 99).[34] In a last ditch effort to turn the voting tide *The Judge* desperately tied Cleveland pictorially not only to Mormonism and the aforementioned issues, but also to "Whiskey Interests," "Colored Orphan Asy-

32. *The Judge*, 25 October 1884, p. 3.
33. *Jingo*, 17 September 1884, p. 20.
34. Ibid., 22 October 1884, p. 112.

Fig. 94. "The Only Sure Way." *The Daily Graphic*, 6 December 1883.

Fig. 95. "Unequal to the Task." *The Daily Graphic*, 12 December 1883.

Fig. 96. "Would this Solve the Question?" *The Daily Graphic*, 9 March 1882.

Fig. 97. "Congenial Company." Drawn by Thomas Worth for *The Judge*, 25 October 1884.

Fig. 98. "We are with the Democratic Party because its Tendency is to Restore Individual Rights.—*Mormon Bishop Hart*." *Jingo*, 17 September 1884.

lums," "Andersonville," "The Tweed Ring" and "Anti–Abraham Lincolnism."[35]

Of course, Cleveland and the Democratic party also had cartoon support, especially from the Democratically partisan *Puck*. In fact, Cleveland attributed much of his success to Bernard Gillam's series of cartoons portraying James G. Blaine as the "Tattooed Man."[36]

The political battle of the weeklies continued after the election. *Puck* and Gillam cast President Cleveland as Hercules wielding the club of "honest legislation" against an assortment of foes (Fig. 100). One of these foes was Mormonism, represented by a grotesque male, toothless, heavyset, hands forming as claws, unangelic wings protruding from his back, phony halo hovering uneasily over his head.[37] Later Gillam turned from Hercules to the giant Gulliver as a symbol of Grover Cleveland "taking possession of the enemy's [Republican party] fleet and [depriving] them of their strength."[38] The text amplified the meaning of the double-page color print.[39]

> He [Cleveland] has taken from their sloop of war "Mormon Question," their swift cruiser "Silver Question," their frigates "Sound Money" and "Tariff Reform," their unarmed light ship "Harmony Between North and South," and their double-turreted, heavy-armored, iron-clad ram "Friend of the Negro." And what is more, he has proved that these vessels now belong, by right of capture, to the Democratic party. And still better, he has taken the dummy guns out of them, put in cannon that will shoot, and he is going to make them speak on and after this date. That's what Mr. Cleveland has done with the war-ships of the enemy.

---

35. *The Judge*, 1 November 1884, pp. 8–9.

36. See Stephen Becker, *Comic Art in America* (New York: Simon and Schuster, 1959), p. 296. Ironically, Bernard Gillam voted for James G. Blaine.

37. *Puck*, 18 February 1885.

38. Ibid., 17 June 1885, pp. 248–49.

39. Ibid., p. 242.

Fig. 99. "The Dying Tree." *Jingo*, 22 October 1884.

Fig. 100. "Foes in His Path.—The Herculean Task Before Our Next President." Drawn by Victor Gillam for *Puck*, 18 February 1885.

Fig. 101. "A Terror that He Doesn't Seem to Tackle." *The Judge*, 15 August 1885, drawn by D. Mac.

Fig. 102. "Hit 'Em Again." *The Judge*, 9 January 1886, drawn by D. Mac.

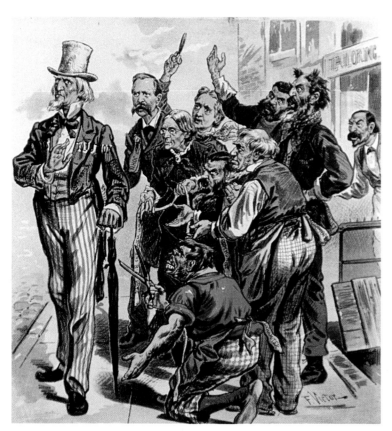

Fig. 103. "The Old Coat. *Chorus of Tailors*—'Hadn't you better let
us repair that coat: It's too old-fashioned for these go-ahead times.'
Uncle Sam—'The coat is good enough for me, and will last at least
another hundred years!' *The Judge*, 3 September 1887. Drawn
by F. Victor Gillam.

Fig. 104. "16-to-1." Drawn by Zim for *The Judge*,
12 September 1896.

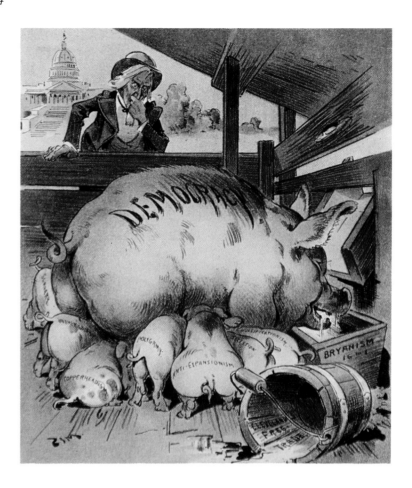

Fig. 105. "The Mother of Them All." *The Judge*, 30 October 1899, drawn by Zim.

Puck was thus trying to increase the psychological distance between Cleveland and Mormonism. At the same time, *The Judge* was attempting to narrow the gap, continuing the guilt by association it had promoted during the campaign. The strategy appears, for example, in a colorful lithograph published on 15 August 1885 (Fig. 101).[40] A timid Cleveland stands with an undersized dogcatcher net while the Mormon bulldog chews on the American flag. The caption reads, "A Terror that He Doesn't Seem to Tackle." The driver of the "National Dog-Pound Van" is Daniel S. Lamont, Cleveland's private secretary, a reminder of the common joke among journalists that if action from Cleveland were desired, you had to see Lamont.

Two more lithographs on political themes relevant to Mormonism appeared in *The Judge* before Cleveland left office. The first, in anticipation of more sweeping legislation, showed Senator Edmunds in the act of again striking the "Mormon Bluebeard" (Fig. 102).[41] The other lithograph, the work of F. Victor Gillam, showed Mormonism, Anarchism, Socialism, Dynamite-

40. *The Judge*, 15 August 1885, p. 1.
41. Ibid., 9 January 1886, p. 1. The date on the lithograph is incorrect. It should be 1886, not 1885.

ism, Communism, Prohibition, and Women's Rights threatening the Constitution of the United States (Fig. 103).[42] The Mormon has a firm handclasp with the communist. Both illustrations reflect the grim guilt-by-association humor used against Mormonism.

For *Puck* turnabout was fair play when Benjamin Harrison succeeded Grover Cleveland. Just a few short months into Harrison's term of office *Puck* complained that the new president was ignoring character and competence in his political appointments. C. J. Taylor, a cartoonist for *Puck*, stressed this view by depicting "Harrisons from Nauvoo" (Mormons), "Harrisons from Chinatown," "Harrisons from Coonville" (blacks), a "Mrs. Levi Harrison" (Jewish), "Pocahontas Harrison" (native American), the "O'Harrisons" (Irish), and "Harrisons from Deadwood" coming for their political spoils.[43] It was the same old refrain: innocent, unpopular groups were exploited for political purposes.

Nevertheless, by the time Harrison came to office in 1889, the vexing Mormon problem was well on its way to solution after dogged enforcement of anti-polygamy statutes by the federal government had led to the announcement that no more plural marriages would be authorized. The announcement neutralized Mormonism as a political issue for a time and sent cartoonists scurrying after other topics.

In 1896 when William Jennings Bryan advocated a return to the 16-to-1 ratio of silver to gold, Eugene "Zim" Zimmerman could not resist showing "The 16 to 1 movement in Utah"— an old Mormon male flanked by eight wives to his right and left (Fig. 104).[44]

The Roberts and Smoot Cases

When questions were raised about the propriety of B. H. Roberts representing the new state in Congress, political cartoons turned again to Mormonism.[45] "Zim" capitalized on the renewed salience of the topic and William Jennings Bryan's second try for the presidency in *The Judge* cartoon.[46] Uncle Sam holds his nose against the stench of the political pigpen containing a huge pig symbolic of the Democratic party. The sow, "Mother of them all," is eating slop out of the trough "Bryanism

42. Ibid., 3 September 1887, p. 1. Contrary to this image, Mormon theology views the Constitution of the United States as a sacred document of divine origin. Susan B. Anthony, Belva Lockwood, and John Pierce St. John are the only identifiable personalities in the picture. The women, of course, represented Women's Rights and St. John was an ardent prohibitionist.

43. *Puck*, 27 February 1889, pp. 216–17.

44. *The Judge*, 12 September 1896, p. 176.

45. See Chapter 3.

46. *The Judge*, 30 October 1899.

Fig. 106. *"Uncle Sam*: Now There's a Merger that Will Stand Looking Into." Pen-and-ink drawing by F. T. Richards for *Philadelphia North American*, 28 August 1907.

16 to 1" while nursing the piglets "Polygamy," "Slavery," "Unamericanism," "Copperheadism," "Anti-expansionism," "Secession," and "Nullification" (Fig. 105).

Political cartoons resulting from Reed Smoot's election to the Senate were explored in Chapter 3.[47] President Theodore Roosevelt had advised Utah against sending a church apostle, but when Smoot called the President's action "unprecedented interference," Roosevelt backed down on the matter. Cartoonists linked the toothy, walrus-like countenance of Roosevelt with Mormonism.[48]

As a concluding sample from this era, we take a creative product from the work of Frederick T. Richards. Richards saw in Mormonism a vehicle to deal humorously with Roosevelt's penchant for monopoly legislation. "Now There's a Merger that Will Stand Looking Into," declared Uncle Sam (Fig. 106). The pen-and-ink drawing took on Roosevelt and Mormonism good-naturedly but effectively. The tattered stovepipe hat, checkered pants, enormous beard, comic expressions, ludicrous fashion, and numbers designating sequence of marriages and offspring—all of the elements of first-rate political caricature were there.[49]

Political cartooning at the expense of the Mormons was not over, but early in the twentieth century it died out as a means of trying to smear national candidates or parties. Since Mormons were found in both parties efforts to link them to just one party were unconvincing. The effective end of polygamy and the apparent accommodation to national norms made them far less useful as symbols of depravity and social degradation. Although charges of Mormon influence in politics continued from time to time, this was mainly an issue within the state of Utah.[50] Mormonism had lost most of the symbolic value that for fifty years had allowed it to serve as a weapon in the arsenal of political caricature.

47. See Chapter 3.

48. The anti-Mormon *Salt Lake Tribune* claimed in a cartoon that the Mormon church slandered Teddy Roosevelt by proclaiming his friendship. See 13 December 1905 and 23 September 1906.

49. For a discussion of the characteristics of fine political caricature, see Nevins and Weitenkampf, *A Century of Political Cartoons*, pp. 9–10.

50. Political cartooning during the brief revival of anti-Mormonism associated with the American Party, from 1905 to 1911, will repay study, as will representations of Mormonism in elections after that date. But not only does our own study end in 1914, which we see as a natural terminus, but also we are confident that the use of Mormonism as a subject by cartoonists is never again what we have described here—a means of discrediting national parties and presidential candidates throughout the nation.

7. Double Jeopardy: Visual Images of Mormon Women

In the nineteenth and early twentieth centuries pictorial prejudice toward women, as well as toward ethnic, racial and religious groups, was typically American.[1] Although the media images of women were usually more subtle than the prevailing stereotypes of unpopular American minorities, they were no less effective in delineating the socially sanctioned province of women and punishing by ridicule any deviations from these accepted conventions of behavior.[2] For women belonging to an unpopular ethnic or religious group there was double jeopardy. They could be maligned for the supposed attributes of their gender, the real or imagined characteristics of their group, or a more complex interaction between these factors. The image of the tyrannical Irish servant-girl, Bridget, or the domineering Irish housewife exemplify how gender and group interacted to fix an unfavorable image.[3]

Mormon women were as vulnerable as any women of this period to negative stereotyping. Although the literary dimensions of the subject have received some attention, no one has yet examined visual images of Mormon women.[4] Since the visual portrayals undoubtedly influenced American public opinion, perhaps more profoundly than verbal characterizations, they deserve analysis.

The pictorial images of Mormon women consisted of a complex collage of mental, moral, social, emotional, and physical elements. For purposes of analysis we are grouping the different elements into two general categories. The first concentrates on the perceived effect Mormonism had upon its female constituents. The system was portrayed as victimizing women, attracting undesirable female specimens to the fold, or some combination of the two. The second category exploited general stereotypes of women and applied them to the special case of Mormonism. Although there is unavoidable overlapping in these categories and the different images used to convey their message, they are sufficiently discriminant to warrant separate discussion. Several distinct images emerge from the analysis.

---

1. For example, see John Appel and Selma Appel, "The Grand Old Sport of Hating Catholics: American Anti-Catholic Caricature Prints," *The Critic* (November–December 1971):50–58.

2. Eleanor Flexner, *Century of Struggle* (New York: Atheneum, 1974).

3. John J. Appel, "From Shanties to Lace Curtains: The Irish Image in *Puck*, 1876–1910," *Comparative Studies in Society and History* 13 (October 1971):365–75.

4. Several studies have appeared on images of Mormon women, but none concentrating on visual images. See Claudia Bushman, *Mormon Sisters: Women in Early Utah* (Cambridge, Mass.: Emmeline Press, 1976).

Fig. 107. "Pure White 'Mormon Immigration' On the Atlantic Coast. More *cheap* 'help-mates' for Mr. Polygamist." *Harper's Weekly*, 25 March 1882. Drawn by Thomas Nast.

Mormon Women as Commodities

To judge from many of the pictures, Mormonism provided no happiness for its women. Quite common were representations showing them being treated as though they had only instrumental value—as role occupants rather than humans. "I found a parody on the religion of the Bible and of the Koran," wrote one traveler, "sanctioning and prescribing the treatment of women, not as intellectual human beings, but as mere human toys."[5] The assertion that they were treated as less than human was reinforced by animal imagery. "Brigham's whole herd of women" were "turned out into the enclosure to be aired" (*Harper's Weekly*, 9 October 1858). "A carload of female recruits," "a fresh supply of wives" (as in fresh fish), "a cargo of recruited women," "a new lot of English female converts," and "recruiting inmates for the seraglios of Utah" further expressed depersonalization. When someone asked, "Where's Brother Jones?" someone else replied, "Gone East to replenish his fall stock" (*The Argonaut*, 21 November 1904). Thomas Nast, the celebrated cartoonist for *Harper's Weekly*, 25 March 1882, captured the essence of the theme by showing immigrant Mormon females being herded off a ship with signs around their necks designating their respective roles—cook, chambermaid, waitress, nurse, laundress, and seamstress (Fig. 107).

Often women were shown as something between sexual objects and cattle. A man might be shown dickering with a father over the "purchase" of his daughters—assessing their age and beauty to see how many he could bargain for with the livestock he was willing to trade.[6] An illustration depicting the "arrival of an installment of wives at Salt Lake" shows comely and fashionably dressed young ladies alighted from a train. One poses prettily while a prosperous looking gentleman holds her face by the chin and appears to be sizing up her physical attributes.[7] Similarly, another cartoon shows a father consenting to give away two attractive daughters with the stipulation that a third, an ugly duckling type, be thrown in on the deal (*Life*, 21 August 1913).

In the popular media, these Mormon women once married continued to receive affronts to their individuality. Insensitive or forgetful husbands could not keep their wives straight and even failed to recognize a spouse now and then. In this vein, an illustrator for *Puck* pictured an old businessman chastizing his office boy for not taking down his wife's "name and number" when

5. *Appleton's Handbook of American Travel, Western Tour* (New York: D. Appleton and Company, 1872), p. 260.

6. Maria Ward, *The Mormon Wife* (Hartford, Conn., 1873), p. 325.

7. Alfred Trumble, *The Mysteries of Mormonism* (New York: Police Gazette, 1882), p. 12.

Fig. 108. "Bringing Home the Fifth Wife—A Sketch in Mormondom." Drawn by Tavernier and Frenzeny for *Harper's Weekly*, 2 January 1875.

she called (see Fig. 129). A ridiculous extension of this idea appeared in *Carl Pretzel's Weekly*:

> A Mormon editor of Salt Lake City has the following in a recent issue of his paper: The unknown woman who was killed at this place about three months ago by the cars proved to be one of the wives of the editor of this paper! A new count appears to have revealed the fact![8]

The Embattled Mormon Woman

It was not simply male versus female, for, according to a constantly reiterated theme, Mormon wives were engaged in horrendous domestic strife, new versus established wife, young versus old, and the husband in the middle. The arrival of a "new wife" was a situation whose emotional dynamics were frequently explored in visual representations. The husband usually enters the home with the new wife, young and well dressed, on his arm (Fig. 108). The three or four other wives, older and in everyday housedresses, all stare at her. The children hide behind their mothers or show their curiosity by staring also. The new wife is shy or apprehensive, the older wives fearful, resentful, or angry—and sometimes surprised. The emotional tension is always high.[9]

Mormon males were shown placing a high premium on youth. This prompted a warning to the young: "In time the present new-comer will have to take her place in the background in favor of some younger and more fascinating charmer."[10]

8. *The Argonaut*, 31 January 1885, reprinted from *Carl Pretzel's Weekly*.

9. Ann Eliza Young, *Wife No. 19, Or the Story of a Life in Bondage* (Hartford, Conn.: Dustin, Gilman & Co., 1876), p. 297; J. W. Buel, *Metropolitan Life Unveiled; Or the Mysteries and Miseries of America's Great Cities* . . . (St. Louis: Historical Publishing Co., 1882), p. 450. For illustration see *Harper's Weekly*, 2 January 1875.

10. *Harper's Weekly*, 2 January 1875, p. 10.

Fig. 109. "Better Halves in Utah. The First Shall Be Last and the Last Shall Be First." *Life*, 15 August 1912, drawn by Orron Lowell.

A clever cartoon on "Better Halves in Utah" depicted age discrimination by showing a husband followed, in order of age, by five wives (Fig. 109). A caption commented, "The first shall be last and the last shall be first."

The Impoverished Mormon Woman

Mormon women were often portrayed as victims of poverty. An article on the "Dreadful State of Women" noted: "There are among this people . . . hundreds of females who have not a shift to their backs, and in instances not a few their outer garments (alias tatters and rags) are insufficient to conceal their nakedness as they go about the house" (*Harper's Weekly*, 25 September 1858). To convey this predicament visually artists would show a poor, usually polygamous rural family whose members sit or stand outside a small rough cabin.[11] An inside view of a poor Mormon home might show a small, cluttered room with women getting in each other's way, several children underfoot, and a tattered sheet hung from the ceiling to separate the beds in the sleeping area.[12] In one illustration a woman sits on a bare chair in an almost empty room holding one hand over her sad face and comforting her children with the other as they beg her for bread.[13] The effects of their harsh existence often showed on the faces of these women. Tired, worn-out features and sour expressions were common.[14] Even young girls, perceived as see-

11. Buel, *Metropolitan Life*, p. 478.

12. Mrs. T. B. H. Stenhouse, *Exposé of Polygamy in Utah: A Lady's Life Among the Mormons* (New York: American News Co., 1872), p. 154.

13. Buel, *Metropolitan Life*, p. 467.

14. Jennie Anderson Froiseth, *The Women of Mormonism; Or the Story of Polygamy* (Detroit: C. G. G. Paine, 1882), p. 184.

ing no possibility of an improvement in their condition, looked dejected and dispirited.[15]

The Subjugated Mormon Woman

Especially popular was the image of the Mormon woman as an overworked slave, tyrannized by her husband. In some scenes male domination was unmistakable. The husband points out to his new bride a sign over the door reading "I Rule the Ranch"— with pistols, club, whip, and skull and crossbones mounted below it. The bride draws back aghast.[16] In other pictures the wife is shown as an all-purpose slave, toiling over huge tubs of laundry,[17] or beating the oxen and trying to lead them along while her husband, swigging from a bottle, rides in the wagon (Fig. 110).[18]

In several pictures the husband holds a whip. The women, like slaves, labor in the fields.[19] One picture, captioned "Wives as slaves toiling under the lash of the whip," shows several immigrant-convert-wives digging and scratching in the ground or carrying heavy sacks over their shoulders. Attached to their ankles are balls and chains bearing the labels "sealed" and "ignorance." Nearby sits the husband, a whip labeled "intimidation" tucked under his arm. He is reading a sheet titled "Account money saved in farmhands."[20] The effort to draw a parallel with southern black slavery, already patent enough, is reinforced in this picture by a black man who carries a scroll labeled "emancipation" and who casually looks upon their labors. By implication Mormon women were even worse off than the enslaved blacks.

Mormon women were often pictured either fleeing from or being deserted by their husbands. One common scene shows the husband standing in the doorway, pointing his finger at the offending wife as he sends her out of the house (Fig. 111). She clutches a small bundle of belongings and covers her face with her hand.[21] In a similar picture the ejected woman is an older woman, while the husband in the doorway embraces a younger, more pleasing wife.[22] Another favorite scene is the woman either driven or fleeing from her home in a snowstorm, usually carrying a baby and accompanied by two or three small

Fig. 110. "A Modern Home Ruler," From *The Mysteries of Mormonism* by Alfred Trumble published in 1882.

---

15. Kate Tannatt Woods, *Across the Continent* (Boston: Lothrop Publishing Company, 1897), p. 189.

16. Trumble, *The Mysteries of Mormonism*, p. 38.

17. Young, *Wife No. 19*, p. 532.

18. Trumble, *The Mysteries of Mormonism*, p. 38.

19. Ibid., p. 18.

20. William Jarman, *Uncle Sam's Abscess or Hell Upon Earth* (Exeter, Engl., 1884), frontispiece. This print appeared originally in *Leslie's Weekly*, 11 March 1882, cover.

21. Young, *Wife No. 19*, p. 31.

22. Trumble, *The Mysteries of Mormonism*, p. 58.

Fig. 111. "Sending the Offending Wife Away." From *The Mysteries of Mormonism* by Alfred Trumble published in 1882.

children. They may be heavily bundled or without any coats at all. The woman's face, if visible, shows despair and hopelessness.[23] The similarity to the pathetic flight of Liza in *Uncle Tom's Cabin* would not be lost on nineteenth-century readers.

The Worldly Mormon Woman

Periodically illustrators painted lurid scenes of lust and debauchery. This was the Mormon-household-as-harem motif, but Mormon women might, in the imagination of the public, have been enjoying this aspect of their experience. Several pictures fed this imagination by showing enthusiastic female participants. Obviously anything that suggested orgies or sex would have been titillating to the mass audience. For this purpose baptism and temple ceremonies were occasionally portrayed pictorially and of course distorted in order to show attractive, seminude female figures.[24] Even light-hearted cartoon scenes such as the oversized bed of Brigham Young or the popular separately published print, "Last Into Bed Put Out the Light," (Fig. 36) could carry suggestive overtones. Though the most common theme of the worldly Mormon woman was lust, other infamous patterns of behavior, including murder, torture and sadism, were occasionally part of the repertoire.

The Uncultured Mormon Woman

Ignorant, lower-class, and backward women were the essential components of this category. Rarely were Mormon women considered as gifted with strong minds. When a writer for *Harper's Weekly* visited Salt Lake City, he was "amused at the idea of strong-minded women" being in Utah. He conceded there were a few like Eliza R. Snow, who was active in expressing Mormon women's views about themselves, but then he resorted to ridicule: "I asked 'if there were any connection between her homely face, her strong mind, her age and her name of Miss?'"[25] A classical pictorial representation appeared in *Wild Oats* by the noted illustrator Edward Jump.[26] The pipe-smoking, unrefined, pregnant wife vividly portrays the stereotype (Fig. 25).

Detractors explained that conversion to Mormonism was a means for poor, unintelligent immigrant girls to come to Amer-

---

23. William Jarman, *The Mountain Meadows Massacre and the Confession and Execution of the Mormon Bishop John D. Lee* (n.p., n.d.), p. 6.

24. Trumble, *The Mysteries of Mormonism*, pp. 14, 22, 52, and frontispiece. See also J. B. Franklin, *The Mysteries and Crimes of Mormonism* (London, n.d.), pp. 378–79; and Buel *Metropolitan Life*, p. 369.

25. *Harper's Weekly*, 10 October 1857, p. 649. Eliza R. Snow was an intellectual and spiritual leader of Mormon women. In 1870 she and 5,000 other Mormon women gathered in the Tabernacle in Salt Lake City to oppose antipolygamy legislation. This Great Indignation Meeting was followed by other gatherings among Mormon women throughout Utah.

26. *Wild Oats*, 28 March 1872, p. 16.

ica. Dozens of pictures showed the young females arriving on the ship, being examined by villainous polygamists, journeying to the West, and being sent out to settlements (Figs. 64, 67). Although such women need not be mentally inferior, it was easy to picture them as lower-class, uneducated people. The middle-class audience that read the illustrated weeklies throughout the country might very well feel some sympathy for these "victims" of a nefarious system, but it would be rather natural for the widespread nativist sentiment, which saw immigrants as an inferior group of uneducated rejects, to rub off on Mormonism and on Mormon women in particular.[27]

In some ways the most interesting explanation of Mormonism's appeal was pseudoscientific. A journalist for *Harper's Weekly* reported on 10 October 1857:

> I could not listen to the sermon for looking at those wretched and deluded women, who, first enslaved by this atrocious fanaticism, were then swayed at the will of their prophet. I asked myself what new principle of mental magnetism or psychology could fully explain their submission and his power.

The stock psychological answers were supplied by the theories of the day—mesmerism, phrenology, physiognomy, and humoral psychology.[28] Such explanations were quite consistent with the ideas already expressed; lower-class, uneducated females would be particularly susceptible to such devices.

The Unsightly Mormon Woman

Sometimes several motives combined to stimulate a certain theme. Explaining how women could be attracted to such a system as Mormonism, demonstrating the presumed horrible consequences of polygamy, illustrating the claim of some physicians or scientists,[29] entertaining by making the subject ludicrous —all of these combined to encourage portrayals of Mormon women as unsightly physical specimens. And there were literary parallels that evoked laughter at the expense of the Mormon women. Humorist Bill Nye's description is one of the harshest:

> I thought I had seen homely women before, but today was reserved for me a spectacle of Mormon hideousness that will haunt me always. In my opinion, polygamy carries its own punishment along with it.

27. See note 6, above.

28. Gary L. Bunker and Davis Bitton, "Some Antecedents of Psychology and the Legitimization of Stereotypes," unpublished paper presented to the annual convention of the American Psychological Association, San Francisco, 29 August 1977.

29. J. H. Beadle, for example, saw the deleterious effects of polygamy in the "strange dullness of moral perception, a general ignorance and apparently inherited tendency to vice." Quoted in Kimball Young, *Isn't One Wife Enough?* (New York: Henry Holt and Co., 1954), p. 24.

Fig. 112. "A Mormon Family out for a Walk." Illustration from John D. Sherwood's *The Comic History of the United States* published in 1870.

It is sufficient punishment for the men to stay in the house with the warty creatures they call their wives.[30]

Something similar to the above account, a motley crew of assorted fat, tall, "warty creatures," appeared in a *Comic History of the United States* (Fig. 112).[31] Note the inclusion of black and oriental types in the Mormon family, another strategy to disparage by highlighting physical differences.[32]

All of the visual motifs examined to this point might be considered as anti-Mormon rather than anti-women. The real target of the criticism, in other words, may have been Mormonism as a system. As one comic writer put it, in the dialectical humor fashionable at the time: "Der Mormon relitchion is pilt on der ruin and disgrace of voomans und der wreck uf decency" (*The Judge*, 22 August 1885). These are the kinds of women that Mormonism attracts, and this is what Mormonism does to its women—this was probably the prime thrust as it was understood by the cartoonists and writers. But this larger intention was small comfort to the Mormon women, for they were scarcely being flattered.

Also available to the illustrators were negative stereotypes of women in general. Familiar for many generations in American and European society, these traditional images took on an air of novelty as they were adapted to portraying Mormon plural wives. It was not new to show women as fickle and flirtatious, as acquisitive and domineering, as crotchety mother-in-law, or as unlovely, "pushy" women's rights activists, but all of these in their Mormon variants assumed an exotic aspect and renewed their humor in the new setting.

Unlike the images discussed, this category tended to shift the burden of interpersonal difficulty in polygamous marriage squarely onto the shoulders of women. One woman was bad enough in a marriage, two or more incomparably worse. Multiple wives were harbingers of multiple male woes.[33] One verse, from a larger poem describing Brigham Young's encounter with Saint Peter at the pearly gates, underscores the spirit of this general category.

---

30. *The Argonaut*, 8 October 1881, p. 2, reprinted from the *Laramie Boomerang*.

31. John D. Sherwood, *The Comic History of the United States* (Boston: Fields, Osgood and Company), p. 452.

32. For another example of the identication of Mormons with other minorities see *Life*, 28 April 1904, p. 404.

33. An editorial in one of the humorous weeklies actually saw Mormonism as a challenge to this stereotype. "The strenuous exertions made by Mormondom to establish the right to contract polygamous marriages knocks the bottom clear out of one of the most popular superstitions of the day—we refer to the belief that man, as a rule, finds one wife to be so much of a nuisance that two or three of them would render life intolerable." *The Wasp*, 25 January 1879.

"Who's there" asked Pete
"Only Brigham Young" said the man with a humble grin.
"Nineteen wives," mused Pete.
"Well you've had your hell, I guess we may let you in!"[34]

Several images have contributed to this multiple wife-multiple woe conception.

The Fickle, Flirtatious Mormon Woman

At least as early as the Utah War, Mormon females were portrayed as especially susceptible to the wiles of gentile men. The solution of the war and the demise of polygamy were often tied to this imagery.[35] This idea appeared in an early cartoon from *Harper's Weekly* on 22 May 1858 (Fig. 12).

Thirty years later when the Mormon right to vote was denied by anti-polygamy legislation and non-Mormons gained political control of Salt Lake City, the image resurfaced. Old Mormon males "with a super-abundance of young wives" were "amazed to see the gallant Gentiles picking the prettiest from the flock" (*The Wasp*, 22 February 1890). Actually the image kaleidoscopically recurred in different forms and colors. When the Japanese ambassador to the United States visited Salt Lake City in the 1870s, a cartoonist for *Leslie's Weekly* pictured overly anxious Mormon females soliciting the ambassador's attention (24 February 1872, Fig. 26). Other versions saw female flirts attracting males to polygamy—"No wonder a man is a bigamist" (*The Judge*, 15 December 1883).

The Acquisitive Mormon Woman

The fashion-conscious, spendthrift female was magnified by Mormonism. *Life* (5 May 1804) published an abbreviated, fictionalized "Diary of a Mormon." One entry revealed: "Spring openings! Today one of my better sixteenths stole away from me while I was snatching some much-needed sleep and went shopping. I see my finish!" And Hepworth Dixon, after seeing *Harper's Bazaar* for sale in Salt Lake City, was even more explicit. "Whatever might have been possible in an isolated community, where women dressed in calico and sun-bonnets, plural marriage could not exist in company with fashion journals which set wives dressing against each other."[36]

Cartoonists eagerly picked up on the same theme. One cartoon presents "The Only Solution of the Mormon Problem" by showing Mormon wives in a state of ecstatic joy as they see shops that offer for sale perfumes, candies, and the latest fash-

---

34. *The Wasp*, 22 September 1877.

35. See Gary L. Bunker and Davis Bitton, "Illustrated Periodical Images of Mormons, 1850–1860," *Dialogue: A Journal of Mormon Thought* 10 (Spring 1977):82–94.

36. *Harper's Weekly*, 12 October 1889, p. 807.

Fig. 113. "The Only Solution of the Mormon Problem." Drawn by Coffin.

ions (Fig. 113). They paw the poor husband from all sides, emptying his pockets by force. Another polygamous family in the background is seen walking along, the husband heading a file of wives, with two or three of the wives breaking away from the group and starting to run towards the shops they have just noticed from a distance. The message may have been serious enough: polygamy as an institution simply cannot maintain itself once the goods and commodities from the national market become more available in Utah. But with respect to women one could also readily conclude that "women will be women," thus adapting to the Mormon scene an existing negative stereotype of women as frivolous creatures whose materialistic interest in fashions and perfumes dominates their lives.

The Domineering Mormon Woman

Extending the nagging, domineering wife image to Mormonism was predictable. A reporter got the following response from an apocryphal "Senator Gilfeathers" when asked his opinion on the Mormon issue: "He said that one wife was all any man wanted. He had had personal experience himself and knew of what he spoke; and he exhibited a beautiful broom-stick bruise which he had got for coming home late from the club as evidence.[37] Naturally the Mormon husband was the target of multiple broom-wielding wives.[38]

Although the ecclesiastical leadership of the church was usually depicted totally in command, some humorists could not resist the temptation to use the domineering female theme.

37. *The Judge*, 11 March 1882, p. 6.
38. Ibid., 17 December 1881, pp. 8–9.

Joseph F. Smith, surrounded by enormous, formidable women, was caricatured in a *New York World* cartoon of 1904 over the caption "There are Influences Greater than the Government in Utah (Fig. 114).[39] Similarly, a cartoon in the *Minneapolis Journal* pictured B. H. Roberts' three wives with rolling pin, cane, and broom under the clever caption "Roberts' Rules of Order."[40] Some humorous dialogue from *Life* drew a similar conclusion concerning the Robert's case. " 'I see there is some criticism because one of the new Congressmen has three wives.' 'Why should there be?' 'They claim he is controlled by a syndicate.' "[41] As with other facets of the image, it was not a new theme; the traditional woman as shrew was simply taken over and given a fresh twist in the Mormon setting by introducing more women.

The epitome of the assertive, ill-tempered female, a stock figure for centuries, was the mother-in-law. Recognizing that a tried and proven humorous device would be even funnier if there were several such women, the caricaturists introduced many versions of Mormon mother-in-law jokes and cartoons. One such illustration was captioned: "Too Much Mother-in-Law (Fig. 115).[42] There is nothing original about them except the increased number of women pictured.

Some misogynists would combine several images into one as they denounced female suffragists, often portrayed as ill-tempered, domineering viragos or ridiculed as mindless kitchen servants or frivolous followers of fashion.[43] Since Mormon women were already being similarly stereotyped, there was no need to tar them with another brush. Actually they deserved to be identified with the women's movement, at least to some extent, for they had enjoyed the franchise early, agitated to regain it after the Edmunds-Tucker Act of 1887 abolished it, and in other respects identified with national women's causes.[44] These political activities of Mormon women were ridiculed from the first. Giving them the vote, according to *The Argonaut* "is to give to a mob of ignorant, foreign-born females the privilege

Fig. 114. "There are Influences Greater than the Government in Utah." *New York World*, 1904.

Fig. 115. "Too Much Mother-in-Law." Illustration from Alfred Trumble's *The Mysteries of Mormonism* published in 1882.

39. *Salt Lake Tribune*, 27 December 1904, reprinted from *New York World*.

40. Ibid., 25 November 1889, reprinted from *Minneapolis Journal*.

41. *The Argonaut*, 20 February 1899, p. 16, reprinted from *Life*.

42. Trumble, *The Mysteries of Mormonism*, p. 58.

43. Other images appeared infrequently in the popular media such as the talkative Mormon woman. " 'But to my mind,' said the clerical tourist from the East, 'a plurality of wives is unspeakable.' 'Huh,' snorted the good-natured Mormon. 'I never even heard of one wife that was unspeakable.' " *The Argonaut*, 13 July 1907, p. 32, reprinted from *Philadelphia Press*.

44. Beverly Beeton, "Woman's Suffrage in the American West, 1869–1896." Ph.D. dissertation, University of Utah, 1976; and Jean B. White, "Woman's Place Is in the Constitution: The Struggle for Equal Rights in Utah in 1895," *Utah Historical Quarterly* 42 (Fall 1974):344–69.

Fig. 116. "Mormonism is on the Wane in Utah." *Life,* 25 June 1914, drawn by A. B. Walker.

of sending a Representative to Congress."[45] Finally, one cartoon brought the two unpopular causes together visually. Four plain, crotchety women with banners of feminism draped around them were shown attacking a symbolic Mormon male (Fig. 116). It is not clear whether women represented the national movement or the hope that Mormon women would have the pictured effect. The stereotype of feminism was clear—old battle-axes wielding their weapons with man on the run.[46]

Not all of the pictures of Mormon women were negative. Perhaps because it was unconvincing to think that all Mormon women were ugly of feature and unattractive in personality, or perhaps because it would be difficult to enlist support for a crusade to rescue such women, they were sometimes portrayed in a more positive light. When their physical beauty was included as part of the picture, it was done with different emphases and in different contexts. Quite common was the Mormon female as modest, lovely, and desirable. The more chaste, virtuous type of Mormon woman was often the object of seduction attempts, usually by old or at least unattractive men, or by a "missionary" more interested in seducing innocent young girls than in gathering converts.

Some visual renditions even pictured Mormon females as genuinely attractive or dignified without recourse to ulterior motives. Several of the illustrations in *Leslie's Weekly* show well-dressed, attractive women with an air of competence. The wives of Brigham Young, as shown in Fig. 21, "Brigham Young's Family Buying Fish" (5 February 1870) and in Fig. 22, "Reserved Circle in the Mormon Theatre for the Children of Brigham Young" (12 February 1870) are attractive and well dressed. The same year "Mormon Leader with His Last Seal" portrays an older man with a young wife, but neither is cruelly caricatured (12 February, 1870, Fig. 117). These may be members of wealthy families, to be sure, but a larger group was shown in "Mormon Demonstrations in Honor of Daniel Wells" (31 May 1879). It is a demonstration or march of determined women with locked arms; flags are flying and signs bear such slogans as "Women in Favor of Polygamy" (Fig. 118). The accompanying article observed another slogan at the scene: "We care less for the cut of our aprons than the loss of our rights."[47] While the whole incident may well have aroused amusement, amazement, or alarm, the women themselves do not appear as lower-class servant girls, feeble-minded, or immoral trollops; they are well dressed, attractive, and insofar as such traits can be portrayed artistically, intelligent and competent. A final

45. *The Argonaut,* 15 January 1881, p. 9.
46. *Life,* 25 June 1914, p. 1162.
47. *Leslie's Weekly,* 31 May 1879, pp. 213–16.

Fig. 117. "Mormon Leader with His Last 'Seal' in the Mormon Theatre." *Leslie's Weekly*, 12 February 1870.

example printed in the same periodical on 15 February 1870 showed a Mormon farmer and his family—three wives and two children—in an ox-cart returning from Salt Lake City. The subject itself might have been titillating enough, but the women were not subjected to visual maligning.

Similar examples of more realistic or positive representations can be found for the Jews, Irish, native Americans, Chinese, and others, as well as for women in general. The fact remains that all of these were subjected to visual defamation. The same is true of Mormon women.

In conclusion, intolerance of women and Mormons presented special problems for those sharing this double identity. In most cases, the frontal attack against Mormon women was really a broadside assault on their faith. Occasionally the "Mormon problem" was used as a pretext to say something unfavorable about women in general; at other times "femaleness" and "Mormonness" combined to form a powerful caricature of reality.

The Mormons were aware of the unfavorable press they were receiving and did not see it as harmless, for it created a climate of opinion in which punitive legislation could be enacted. Efforts were made to counteract the negative current. One of the reasons for the "indignation meetings" of Mormon women was to present a more favorable image of themselves and their views to the national public. "Were we the stupid, degraded, heartbroken beings that we have been represented, silence might become us," said Eliza R. Snow, sixty-five year old leader of the church's women; "but as women of God, . . . we not only speak because we have the right, but justice and humanity demand

Fig. 118. "Detachment of 400 Mormon Women."
Leslie's Weekly, 31 May 1879.

that we should."[48] Eliza R. Snow attempted to put forward a counter-image, what Gail Farr Casterline has called "onward for Zion" as opposed to "in the toils."[49] In speeches and some writings there was perhaps some success in such a strategy. It would be incorrect to think of these women as helpless in the face of a tidal wave of disapproval. *The Woman's Exponent* proclaimed a positive conception of Mormon women for many years.[50] The positive counter-image had its limitations, however, in that it was essentially verbal and largely localized. In the meantime, anti-Mormon plays and novels continued to mold opinion on the subject.[51] And pictorially, as we have seen, the Mormon women were subjected to a representation that was almost always negative.

The Mormon women were misrepresented in about the same way as women in general, but with a difference: polygamy made it possible to give an added fillip to the unkind portrayals.[52] Perhaps like black women or Irish women, the Mormons were part of the general negative stereotyping of females with an added painful thrust accorded to minority groups. To adapt a phrase used in another connection, Mormon women in the nineteenth century were American women with a difference. And in the pictorial representations at least that difference was an increased burden of ridicule and opprobrium.

48. *Deseret News Weekly*, 19 January 1870.

49. Gail Farr Casterline, " 'In the Toils' or 'Onward for Zion': Images of the Mormon Woman, 1852–1890," Master's thesis, Utah State University, 1974.

50. Carol Cornwall Madsen, "Remember the Women of Zion: A Study of the Editorial Content of the *Woman's Exponent*, a Mormon Woman's Journal," Master's thesis, University of Utah, 1977.

51. Leonard J. Arrington and John Haupt, "Intolerable Zion: The Image of Mormonism in Nineteenth Century American Literature," *Western Humanities Review* 22 (Summer 1968):243–60.

52. Carol Wald, *Myth America: Picturing Women 1865–1945* (New York: 1975).

8. Mischievous Puck And the Mormons

One of the most valuable examples of the twentieth century's new strain of pictorial representations of Mormonism is found in *Puck*, published in New York since 1877.[1] *Puck* had started as a German publication but within a year was appearing in English. Henry Cuyler Bunner produced most of the written commentary, and Joseph Keppler, the founder, did many of the lithographs for the weekly until his death in 1894. "What Fools these Mortals Be!" was the motto and sharp satire the magazine's trademark. It was without peer among the humorous illustrated weeklies of its time, although *The Wasp*, *The Judge*, and *Life* all had their moments.

After 1900 *Puck* cartooned and caricatured Mormonism more than any other weekly. Did the ensuing cartoons defuse some of the animosity, intensify antipathy, or leave mixed effects? How did the cartoon portrayal of Mormonism during this period compare with the pre-Manifesto representations? An analysis of cartoons in this popular and humorous illustrated magazine throws some light on these questions.

Puck's earlier representations of Mormonism were not always gentle, although it must be said that other religions were also targets. In 1877 *Puck* published one of its most popular cartoons which irreverently poked fun at Brigham Young's death (Fig. 37). Other cartoons invidiously symbolized Mormons as snakes (Fig. 80) or black crows in Uncle Sam's eagle's nest (Fig. 43), and dressed Mormons in Turkish costumes (Fig. 44). Such satirical cartoons coupled with slashing political and literary criticism combined to make the magazine popular; its circulation was nearly 90,000 during the nineties, not counting the monthly and quarterly versions that republished the best from *Puck*. As it entered the twentieth century, the magazine was well established, and with a different cast of editors and artists it was ready to take on the foolish mortals of the new century.

Within the four-year period of the Smoot Senate hearings, fifteen cartoons about Mormons appeared in *Puck*. Ironically, although they were doubtless stimulated by the Smoot publicity, only one of them dealt directly with Smoot. This cartoon, the sole exception to the more tolerant, if condescending, mood of twentieth-century *Puck* towards the Mormons, appeared on 27

---

1. See Frank L. Mott, *A History of American Magazines, 1865–1885*, 5 vols. (Cambridge, Mass.: Harvard University Press, 1938), 3:520–32.

Fig. 119. "The Real Objection to Smoot." Drawn by Keppler for *Puck*, 27 April 1904.

Fig. 120. "Out in Salt Lake City. *Elder Heaperholmes—* 'He has been tried by the church and found guilty of bigamy.' Elder Holikuss—'Guilty of bigamy?' *Elder Heaperholmes—* 'That's the judgment. He's been married twice.' " Drawn by Erhart for *Puck*, 20 April 1904.

April 1904 with Joseph Keppler, Jr., as the cartoonist.[2] Keppler's cartoon was closer in spirit to some of the more hostile cartoons of nineteenth-century *Puck*. Entitled "The Real Objection to Smoot," it showed the Senator being wound up with a key by the larger bearded Mormon hierachy lurking behind the scenes and draped with Polgyamy, Mountain Meadows Massacre, Resistance to Federal Authority, Murder of Apostates, Mormon Rebellion, and Blood Atonement (Fig. 119). This was not too gentle.

More typical of the period, however, was the spoofing of a polygamy now seen as more amusing than threatening. Even though cartoonist S. Ehrhart, a prolific contributor to *Puck*, was best known for his caricatures of the apish-faced Irish immigrant and the "light-fingered Negro," he was just as comfortable with the theme of the much-married Mormon.[3] His approach was the same for all of these minorities. Whether Irish, Negro, or Mormon, the unpopular were deftly reduced to unattractive stereotypes. His first of four Mormon cartoons during the new century was a full-page color feature on *Puck*'s cover for 20 April 1904 (Fig. 120). Ehrhart's lighter touch was characteristic of the cartoons about the Mormons which followed in *Puck*.

Cartoons about Mormonism in *Puck* capitalized on the inevitable complexities introduced by polygamy. Two main humorous devices were used: (1) special technological inventions for Mormons and (2) a tongue-in-cheek analysis of human relations within the social structure of polygamy. Let us first look at the inventions.

Inventions for Polygamists

Inventing special devices for Mormons was not really a new idea. Artists of the previous generation had pictured huge, multiple baby buggies, an automatic bathing and dressing machine for the seemingly countless Mormon children, oversized containers of paregoric for ailing Mormon families, and even decorative porcelain and bric-a-brac in the large, economy Utah size. On 21 June 1905 *Puck*'s first twentieth-century invention for Mormonism appeared—a very fat "Mormon Case Watch for the Utah Jewelry Trade" (Fig. 121). In its closed position it

2. On the basis of a content analysis of magazine articles, Jan Shipps has calculated that the image of Mormonism was still negative during the generation following the Manifesto (see "From Satyr to Saint: American Attitudes toward the Mormons, 1860–1960," paper presented at the 1973 meeting of the Organization of American Historians; copy in possession of the authors). She did not, however, attempt to measure fluctuations within the period with any precision, and her categories did not allow her to recognize treatments that, as we have found, though still negative, were but mild ridicule rather than biting criticism.

3. William Murrell, *A History of American Graphic Humor: 1865–1938*, 2 vols. (New York: Cooper Square Publication, 1967), 2:90.

Fig. 121. "Mormon Case Watch for the Utah Jewelry Trade." *Puck*, 21 June 1905, drawn by Erhart.

Fig. 122. "The Automormon Expressly Designed for Family Use in Utah." Drawn by L. M. Glackens for *Puck*, 14 March 1906.

Fig. 123. "Cupid in Utah." Drawn by Gordon Grant. *Puck*, 28 March 1906.

was like other watches except for its unusual thickness. In its open position out came the portraits of several wives, the last, of course, being the youngest and most attractive.

The following year saw the conception of three more inventions. The new age of motor cars led the comic artist Louis M. Glackens to create for publication "The Automormon Expressly Designed for Family Use in Utah" (Fig. 122). A venerable partriarch was at the wheel, while behind in seven rows of seats were enough wives and children to make up a veritable congregation. On the automobile's front was the model name, a most fitting appellation: "The Smoot."

Even Cupid could not be content with the old-fashioned bow and arrow in Mormondom (Fig. 123). Instead he now needed a machine gun. A poor defenseless man is shown being hit by a whole volley of arrows with a dozen or more women standing behind the rapid fire weapon. What makes this cartoon interesting is the substitution of the image of anxious Mormon females in pursuit for the more usual stereotype of the amorous Mormon male. This clever creation appeared 28 March 1906.

The attempt to provide Mormons with new devices continued in the cartoon "Holding Hands in Utah," 22 August 1906, in which the bearded husband manipulates a multiple hand apparatus that reaches out to his various wives (Fig. 124). Note the proximity of the younger wives to the contented old gentleman and the baleful looks of the older, more remotely positioned spouses. The allegedly favored status of younger wives was a favorite cartoon theme.

Laughing at Mormon Families

The second major strategy of the *Puck* humorists was to concentrate on polygamous human relations. The entire sequence of courting, wedding, and honeymoon and the subsequent problems of marriage were satirically treated. Pestering mothers-in-law, forgetting anniversaries, forgetting family members' names, caring for sick children during the night—these situations which had long been exploited in the comic portrayal of marriage and family life were magnified and given new life by polygamy.

Two cartoons with courtship themes were published in 1906. The first, a full-page color cartoon entitled "Midsummer Night Dreams," which appeared on 25 July, showed various styles of courtship in different cities (Fig. 125). In proper Boston the couples held hands at a proper distance. In Philadelphia it was a more tender and closer situation, the young man's arm around his sweetheart. In Chicago, where women were thought to be brazen, she was attacking the delighted youth. At the divorce colony in Dakota (the Reno or Las Vegas of 1906), two couples were seated side by side, with an ingenious switching of spouses. Salt Lake City, not surprisingly, completed the varied picture of "love, American style" by showing the young man being kissed and nuzzled from three sides. A few months later another cartoonist, Albert Levering, chose a proposal scene portraying a

Fig. 124. "Holding Hands in Utah." *Puck*, 22 August 1906, drawn by Gordon Grant.

Fig. 125. "Midsummer Night Dreams." *Puck*, 25 July 1906.

Fig. 126. "A Mormon Version of It. *The Coy Young Utah Thing*—'But are you sure you won't feel the extra expense—if I *should* say yes?' *Elder Studdorse (fervently)*—'My dear there isn't the slightest doubt—twelve can live as cheaply as one.' " Drawn by Albert Levering for *Puck*, 3 October 1906.

Fig. 127. "A Quiet Wedding in Utah: There were present only the immediate families of the bride and groom. —*Salt Lake Society News*." Drawn by L. M. Glackens for *Puck*, 18 April 1906.

bearded Mormon suitor on his knees assuring his prospective bride, "My dear, there isn't the slightest doubt—twelve can live as cheaply as one" (Fig. 126).

Courtship, of course, eventually led to the wedding altar. L. M. Glackens (18 April 1906) used this setting to contrive one of the wittiest images in the history of cartooning Mormons. There was striking incongruity between the caption—"A Quiet Wedding in Utah: There were present only the immediate families of the bride and groom"—and the drawing, which depicted a capacity crowd filling not only the main floor of a large hall but the two balconies as well (Fig. 127). By juxtaposing two incompatible thoughts, verbal and visual, Glackens created what Arthur Koestler has called "bisociative shock," the essence of humor.[4]

If Mormon courtship was sometimes idealized by imaginative illustrators, the images of marriage among the Mormons redressed the imbalance. Even the honeymoon was beset with problems. On 16 May 1906 Fred E. Lewis drew a chagrined, newly-married Mormon couple at the train unexpectedly joined by the husband's other wives, who said, "This makes your fifth wedding trip, Pa; and as we've only had one apiece, we thought we'd come along with you and Tootsie-Wootsie."

The mother-in-law theme was not very original either in general or for Mormons in particular. However, it was then, as now, effective material for the humorist. Ehrhart drew a polygamist husband seated on the porch surrounded by eight attractive, happy wives. Coming up the walk toward the house are several militant, crotchety older women befitting the mother-in-law stereotype (Fig. 128). Dropping the newspaper (*The Daily Bigamist*) in amazement, the husband says, "Shades of Joseph Smith! What the * * * !!" In "gentle chorus" his wives reply: "Only a surprise for you, dearie. Our mothers have come to spend a month with us."

Another old theme was refurbished and returned to action. Brigham Young had often been the subject of earlier cartoons poking fun at his supposed inability to recognize one of his wives or children.[5] Alexander Graham Bell's telephone, by now a standard part of American life, supplied a new social context for an old idea. The office boy announced, "Your wife wants you

4. Arthur Koestler, *The Act of Creation* (New York: Dell Publishing Company, 1975), pp. 91–92.

5. For an early version of this theme see *Harper's Weekly*, 21 February 1857: "I am told by an eye-witness of the scene, that Brigham, walking down the street, a few day since, met a little boy returning from the mountainside with a few cows, which he had been herding. Struck with something in his appearance, the Prophet stopped and called out, 'Here Sonny! Tell me, now, whose son you are.' The little curly-headed urchin answered, 'Ma tells me I'm Brother Young's son, but you ought to know who I am.' The seer knew not his own child!"

on the phone, sir." The proverbial Mormon, seated at his desk and surrounded by pictures of wives numbers one through eight, answers: "Boy, how many times must I tell you to get the name and number of the person who calls up?" Clutter on the desk and the office floor adds to the negative image (Fig. 129).

Thirty years of illustrating Mormons off and on in *Puck* ended with the seating of Senator Reed Smoot in 1907. Three cartoons during the last year of the Smoot hearings put their final touches on the Mormon image. The first, published on 9 January 1907, parodied polygamy by having "Elder Studdorse" invite a friend to his silver, tin, and wooden anniversaries within a two-week period. The surname Studdorse, borrowed by Ehrhart from one of Albert Levering's earlier cartoons (Fig. 126), served as an obvious collective symbol for lust to characterize the stereotyped Mormon behavior pattern. Other Mormon names in the cartoons—Elder Muchmore, Elder Heaperholmes, Elder Holikuss, Mr. Mormondub, Obadiah, Tootsie-Wootsie, and Elder Saltlake—did not carry the same connotation of lust but did help to turn their subjects into figures of ridicule. Similar motives were responsible for the labeling of other minority groups (e.g., Rastus, Aunt Jemima, and Sambo).[6]

On 13 March 1907 J. S. Pughe presented a heavyset, cane-in-hand, apologetic Mormon male at the door of wife No. 5 at 11:30 P.M. Only in Utah would "Obadiah's" explanation for coming home so late be plausible: ". . . whooping cough, measles, teething, mumps and twins." The final cartoon, inspired by the forthcoming Halloween celebration, appeared on 23 October 1907. With the help of Halloween folklore, Gordon Grant, the artist, saw another chance to make light of polygamy. "On the Halloween night, if one holds up a candle and looks in a mirror, the face of one's future husband or wife will be seen."[7] Sure enough, an eager Mormon male with candle in hand stood in front of a mirror full of attractive, youthful, female faces. The cartooning of Mormons in *Puck* ended on a familiar theme.

How Benign Was the Ridicule?

What were the overall effects of mischievous *Puck*? Were Mormon-gentile tensions increased or was there evidence of accommodation? Based in part on a comparative analysis of cartoons in nineteenth-century *Puck*, we believe that the effects

Fig. 128. "In Salt Lake City." *Puck*, 14 June 1905, drawn by Erhart.

Fig. 129. "In Utah. *New Office Boy.*—'Your wife wants you on the 'phone sir.' *Mr. Mormondub.*—'Boy, how many times must I tell you to get the *name* and *number* of the person who calls up.' " Drawn by Albert Levering for *Puck*, 22 August 1906.

6. See E. D. Palmore, "Ethnophanalisms and Ethnocentrism," *American Journal of Sociology* 67 (January 1962):442–45; and Wilmoth A. Carter, "Nicknames and Minority Groups," *Phylon* 5 (Third Quarter, 1944): 241–45.

7. Several other variations of this theme were part of the folklore of the day. For example, "If you stand in front of a mirror at twelve o'clock on Halloween, the man you are to marry will look over your left shoulder." Wayland Hand, ed., *North Carolina Folklore*, 7 vols. (Durham, N.C.: Duke University Press, 1961), 6:599.

of *Puck* were mixed. On the one hand there is evidence of a reduction in tension and a guarded accommodation. On the other hand there are also elements of apprehension, even hostility, as popularly held stereotypes were distilled in picture form by cartoonists of national stature. Let us first look at the evidence in favor of accommodation.

Twentieth-century *Puck* cartoons of Mormons were on the whole less polemical, less serious, and less personal than those of the preceding generation. With the one exception already noted, there was little advocacy of political or social action against the Mormons. Rather than treating the specifics of the Smoot case, the cartoonists were content to deal with the generalized, though mythical, Mormon. This was a significant departure from the explicit support found in many earlier *Puck* illustrations for legislative, executive, and judicial sanctions against the Mormons. If the more light-hearted spirit of the twentieth-century cartoons was not necessarily a manifestation of outright goodwill, neither was it as heavy as the humor of the past, which had emphasized some of the more destructive elements of the image of Mormons—the subversive, hostile, autocratic, and lascivious Mormon. Other components of these older stereotypes were perpetuated, though, as a rule, not nearly so blatantly. Mormons were more laughable, more harmless. The Mormon as buffoon was at least to some degree more socially assimilable than the Mormon as Destroying Angel or Danite. Only one personalized, pictorial attack appeared in the pages of the *Puck* of the new century, as opposed to several instances in the previous century. A reduction in the number of polemical, serious, and personalized cartoons in twentieth-century *Puck* combined with the disappearance in *Puck* of cartoons with Mormon themes after the seating of Smoot, provide some evidence for accommodative concessions by the national press.[8]

But it would be a mistake to consider the new century's caricature of the Mormons in *Puck* as innocuous. Koestler has reminded us that among the indispensable characteristics of most humor is "an impulse, however faint, of aggression or apprehension," which "may be manifested in the guise of malice, derision, the veiled cruelty of condescension, or merely as an

8. There is also some possibility that relatively nonhostile cartoons may have inhibited some aggression against the Mormons. Some contemporary empirical evidence supports the general idea. See Robert A. Baron and Rodney L. Ball, "The Aggression–Inhibiting Influence of Nonhostile Humor," *Journal of Experimental Social Psychology* 10 (January 1974): 23–33. Of course, there were significant exceptions to a more accommodative humor, especially at the local level. The *Salt Lake Tribune* was as polemical, serious, and personalized as ever. It was easier then, as now, to be benevolent at a distance. One must also remember the other side of the coin: "A chosen people is probably inspiring for the chosen to live among; it is not so comfortable for outsiders to live with." Wallace Stegner, *The Gathering of Zion* (New York: McGraw-Hill, 1971), p. 24.

absence of sympathy with the victim of the joke."[9] Inherent in the comic treatment of Mormons was a mood of condescension. Humor continued to set Mormons apart as a distinct cultural (some even suggested racial) species. Such a difference has been the major pretext for prejudice from the beginning of time. To be sure, humor dressed the hostility in culturally acceptable clothing, protecting the creator and the consumer from charges of malicious intent. But what was thought by many to be benign humor, as in the case of the Sambo and minstrel images portraying blacks,[10] was actually profound tragedy. If the cost exacted from Mormons for being so pictured was not so great as for blacks, the dynamics were the same.

Even when the motives of the illustrator were essentially benevolent, the reader would normally extract meaning from the cartoon consistent with his values and experience. Now most people's direct experience with Mormons had been slight, but for several decades they had been bombarded by anti-Mormon images, conditioning them in a tradition of stereotypic thinking. For most people complex categories of thought about Mormons or Mormonism simply were not available. And the cartoon emphasis on cultural peculiarity did not require complex thinking or subtle differentiation; they could be, and doubtless were, read according to the existing simplistic and distorted images of Mormons.

Puck's twentieth-century influence was thus a curious mixture of gradual accommodation and the perpetuation of some "time-honored" stereotypes of Mormons. *Puck* amused and entertained thousands in its time. Although some of the humor was first rate and brought pleasure even to some Mormons, it also brought disgust and pain. Mischievous *Puck* was just that—mischievous.

9. Koestler, *The Act of Creation,* p. 52.

10. Cf. Joseph Boskin, "Sambo: The National Jester in the Popular Culture," in Gary B. Nash and Richard Weiss, ed., *The Great Fear: Race in the Mind of America* (New York: Holt, Rinehart and Winston, 1970), pp. 165–85.

9. Epilogue

We have tried to write a book that is more than an account of the way Mormons in the last century were depicted in the national press; we have sought to write a book about prejudice and the way prejudice became enthroned in stereotypes. We believe it is not enough to recognize that the stereotyping process is a recurrent device by which the human mind tries to deal with complex reality. Stereotypes, such as those of Mormons which we have studied in this book, do not reflect an effort to reduce that complexity, but instead through distortion and mockery seek to communicate a substantially negative image of groups that are not in the mainstream of the dominant culture. Frequently stereotypes contain an element of humor; sometimes the humor is malicious, sometimes it is good natured, sometimes it is done gracelessly, and sometimes with substantial wit and charm. While some of the different ingredients that make up the jokes and cartoons are amusing, the overall consquences of stereotyping are not. Blacks, Catholics, Jews, Irish, Poles, Chinese—these are only a few of the populations that have suffered abuse resulting from stereotypic thinking. "Men act," said French historian Roland Mousnier, "not according to things as they are but as they think they are." The Mormons, the topic of the present analysis, are another such group. It is by heightening awareness of the process—as this book does by examining the single example of the Mormons—that we will improve the ability to recognize this form of prejudice.

It might be thought that we have been selective, choosing only the most glaringly hostile examples. We think not. True, the Mormons made some efforts from the very beginning to win friends and to promote a positive view of their society.[1] And from the beginning through the entire period covered by the present work there were descriptions of the Mormons by outsiders that were friendly and admiring and some that were objective.[2] To assess the relative influence of the different descriptions that made up society's image of the Mormons would require a sophisticated instrument sensitive to tone as well as to different audiences.[3] While awaiting the scholarship that would allow

1. See Davis Bitton, "American Philanthropy and Mormon Refugees, 1846–1849," *Journal of Mormon History* 7 (1980):63–81.

2. Some examples of descriptions not overtly hostile are included in William Mulder and A. Russell Mortensen, eds., *Among the Mormons, Historic Accounts by Contemporary Observers* (New York: Knopf, 1967).

3. The most significant effort to date is Jan Shipps, "From Satyr to Saint: American Attitudes toward the Mormons, 1860–1960," paper presented at 1973 meeting of the Organization of American Historians; copy in possession of the authors.

nuanced conclusions, we simply pass on our impression that the popular image of Mormons throughout the period covered in our study was overwhelmingly negative.

If that judgment is substantially correct, then the present work may suggest the major explanation. For whatever successes the Mormons enjoyed in gaining individual friends of prominence, in promoting their own publications, and even in winning editorial support of some newspapers, they seem to have missed out almost entirely on finding champions among the writers of fiction and the illustrators of books and magazines. To a degree, of course, even the illustrations could be neutral. Especially during the generation or so from the beginning of illustrated periodicals to the use of photography in mass-produced publications, drawings were often intended merely to record the most obvious external appearances of persons, places, and incidents. But enough is known about these processes to make us aware that by selection and subtle emphasis even apparently neutral illustrations conveyed a message.[4] And the simple fact is that most of the illustrations treating the Mormons were not low-key or objective; they were cartoons and caricatures with an obvious point of view. And that point of view was, with almost monotonous regularity, negative.

All of those who created the stereotypes were not malicious in their intent; some were simply having fun at the expense of the Mormons. Yet in their overall impression the illustrations are unfair. Over and over again what the cartoons fail to convey is any sense of how representative a given characteristic or practice was. If viewers of this material came away with the impression that Mormon males were all bearded ogres, that the only marriage pattern in Mormondom was polygamy, or that the women were without exception disheartened and depressed, they were not getting a well-balanced picture. They were seeing a stereotype made up of a series of component elements each of which was a selective magnification and distortion of reality. The result was not a carefully qualified analysis of the complexity of the Mormon population or the changing texture of the movement from place to place or decade to decade. Stereotyping is by its nature not capable of dealing with complexity; its essence is simplicity. Because of its simplicity it can be widely disseminated and easily absorbed.

Most people in the past received their image of Mormons from portrayals that were selective and caricatured. As far as the public is concerned, it seems almost certain that the anti-

---

4. Many illustrations not included in the present study simply show the terrain in the West emphasizing aridity, bleakness, and a kind of ominous threat, not a complete invention, of course, but a subtle emphasis that allowed the same qualities to rub off on the people and religious group located in that environment.

Mormon plays, novels, and illustrations were the primary channels of communication. The illustrations would have been the single most important shaper of the image of Mormons, especially among those who could not read or who read little. What, we may ask, would we ourselves think about a group if all we knew about it was based on the kind of illustrations discussed in the preceding pages? If it is true, as we think it is, that the great majority of people who viewed these illustrations never came in contact with real Mormons and were never reached by the modest efforts to present a favorable counter-image, it is probably understandable why they thought of this religious movement, when they thought of it at all, in negative terms.

If the Mormons of the nineetenth century made some efforts to present their case in a favorable light, their success then was negligible. They have been far more successful in the present century, as the press and the public have become more discerning in their judgments, and as Mormons have become more adept in using the professional expertise of public relations firms to help create a favorable press.[5] Since a fair amount of negative reporting has continued, perhaps at least we have the relatively healthy situation in which one simplified caricature does not dominate the field. If other groups—Catholics, blacks, riflemen, and countless sponsors of lobbyists—are doing some of the same thing, we may be noting one example of the currents and crosscurrents which enter into opinion making in an open society. The tragedy (and that is not too strong a word from the point of view of the victims) is that some groups have been relatively powerless to counteract a ruthless campaign of stereotyping. If we have in any way contributed to a heightened awareness of the tragedy that ultimately hides behind the thoughtless stereotyping of any group, we will have reached our goal.

---

5. "Marketing the Mormon Image: An Interview with Wendell J. Ashton," *Dialogue: A Journal of Mormon Thought* 10 (Spring 1977): 15–20.

Bibliography

Allen, James B., and Glen M. Leonard. *The Story of the Latter-day Saints.* Salt Lake City: Deseret Book, 1976.

Arrington, Leonard J., and Jon Haupt. "Intolerable Zion: The Image of Mormonism in Nineteenth Century American Literature," *Western Humanities Review* 22 (Summer 1968): 243–60.

Arrington, Leonard J., and Davis Bitton. *The Mormon Experience: A History of the Latter-day Saints.* New York: Alfred A. Knopf, 1979.

Becker, Stephen. *Comic Art in America.* New York: Simon and Schuster, 1959.

Blaisdell, Thomas C., Jr., and Peter Selz. *The American Presidency in Political Cartoons, 1776–1976.* Salt Lake City: Perregrine Smith, 1976.

Casterline, Gail Farr. "'In the Toils' or 'Onward for Zion': Images of the Mormon Woman, 1852–1890." Master's thesis, Utah State University, 1974.

Flake, Chad J., ed. *A Mormon Bibliography, 1830–1930.* Salt Lake City: University of Utah Press, 1978.

Hess, Stephen, and Milton Kaplan. *The Ungentlemanly Art: A History of American Political Cartoons.* New York: Macmillan, 1968.

Koestler, Arthur. *The Act of Creation.* New York: Dell Publishing, 1975.

Mott, Frank L. *A History of American Magazines, 1714–1850.* 5 vols. Cambridge, Mass.: Harvard University Press, 1957.

Murrell, William. *A History of American Graphic Humor.* 2 vols. New York: Cooper Square Publishers, 1967. Original ed. 1934, 1938.

Nevins, Allen, and Frank Weitenkampf. *A Century of Political Cartoons.* New York: Charles Scribners Sons, 1944.

Nye, Russell B. *The Unembarrassed Muse: The Popular Arts in America.* New York: Dial Press, 1970.

Shipps, Jan B. "From Satyr to Saint: American Attitudes toward the Mormons, 1860–1960." Unpublished paper in possession of the authors.

Taft, Robert. *Art and Illustrators of the Old West, 1850–1900.* New York: Charles Scribners Sons, 1953.

Tyler, Ron. *The Image of America in Caricature and Cartoon.* Fort Worth, Texas: Amon Carter Museum of Western Art, 1976.

Weitenkampf, Frank. *American Graphic Art.* New York: Macmillan, 1924.

Index

Permissions

Sections from Chap. 1 are repr. by permission of *Dialogue: A Journal of Mormon Thought* 10, no. 3 (Spring 1977): 82–94; Chap. 5 repr. by permission of *Sunstone* 3, no. 6 (Sept.-Oct. 1978): 17–23; Chap. 6 repr. by permission of the Amon Carter Museum, Fort Worth; Chap. 7 repr. by permission of the *Utah Historical Quarterly* 46, no. 2 (Spring 1978): 184–202; Chap. 8 repr. by permission of *Brigham Young University Studies* 18, no. 4 (Summer 1978): 504–19.

Figs. 4 and 35 courtesy of the Western Americana Collection, Beinecke Rare Book and Manuscript Library, Yale University; Figs. 8, 13, 23, 24, 29, 67, 69, 84, 95, 102, 106, and 113 courtesy of the Library of Congress; Figs. 14, 16, 25, and 83 courtesy of the American Antiquarian Society, Worcester, Mass.; Fig. 36 courtesy of the New-York Historical Society; Fig. 45 courtesy of General Research Division, The New York Public Library, Astor, Lenox, and Tilden Foundations; Fig. 56 courtesy of the Harold B. Lee Library, Brigham Young University, Provo, Utah.